101
WAYS TO
RUN A
BUSINESS
PROFITABLY

SUNDAY TELEGRAPH

101
WAYS TO

Edited by
GERALD NICHOLLS
Grant Thornton

RUN A BUSINESS PROFITABLY

Published by the Telegraph Publications
135 Fleet Street, London EC4P 4BL

First published 1985
Second Edition 1986
© Grant Thornton

Grant Thornton cannot assume legal responsibility for the
accuracy of any particular statement in this work.

Printed in Great Britain by
Biddles Ltd, Guildford
Typeset by Sunset Phototype Ltd, Barnet

British Library Cataloguing in Publication Data

Thornton Grant
101 Ways to run a business profitably.
1. Small business – Great Britain – Management
I. Title   II. Sunday Telegraph
658'.022'0941   HD62.7

ISBN 0 86367 089 X

Preface

In recent years, an increasing number of people have taken up the challenge of setting up in business by themselves. Although they may be prepared for hard work and long hours, these factors alone will not guarantee success. Running a business profitably is not easy, as the number of failures show, because owners do not always develop the skills needed to manage the business efficiently despite the fact they have a good service or product to offer.

Expanding a business from a one-man-band to a large company, perhaps operating in different parts of the country, brings its own pressures. There are people to co-ordinate and motivate, product and service ranges to develop and new markets to crack. All growth-orientated businesses, at every stage of development, must continually find ways of facing the problems and opportunities that arise, by organising, planning and controlling their operations effectively.

The aim of *101 Ways to Run a Business Profitably* is to help to make your business – whatever its size – more successful and its future more secure. A team of management consultants from accountants Grant Thornton, under the editorship of the senior consulting partner Gerald Nicholls and his colleagues, give you straightforward guidance on the key issues affecting profitability, drawing on their extensive knowledge and experience.

You will have to find the best ways of applying their advice to your business, but they will help focus your attention on the critical areas.

This is the second issue of this book and I expect it will prove as popular as the other titles in the series. These are *101 Ways of Investing and Saving Money* and *101 Ways of Saving Tax*.

Ian Watson, City Editor, 1986

Contents

1 INTRODUCTION

1 What is a profitable business?

No one should be in business unless he is confident of success; in business the generally accepted measurement of success is profit. Not all businesses will make a profit in the first few years while they are establishing a position in the market, but it is reckless to continue trading when there is no real prospect of at least breaking even in the longer term.

At the simplest level a profitable business is one which has more income than expenditure, but many elements can be brought into this equation. There is no one set of accounting policies and principles which everyone uses for all purposes – thus profits reported in a company's financial accounts will often be very different from the profits the Inland Revenue will accept for tax purposes. Nearly every set of accounts is based to a significant degree on the accountant's judgement.

What level of profits justifies describing a business as profitable? Each owner, employee and investor will have his own opinion, attaching different weight to such factors as security, conditions of employment, expansion and innovation. Few would wish to maximise profit at all cost, but no one would advocate high levels of waste or inefficiency.

The questions in the book are designed to help you know how profitable your business is and, where practicable, improve its performance. However profitable a business is or has been in the past, there are no guarantees of continued success; many profitable businesses ultimately have failed, usually because their products did not keep pace with the market or they did not have enough cash to pay their debts at the right time. Suppliers want their invoices paid promptly and a profitable business will not survive long if it cannot convert enough of its own profits into cash to pay them.

11

A profitable business should be a business with a future. This can only be achieved if the management knows what is happening and is constantly thinking ahead, acting on available information, to put the resources of the business to the most profitable uses.

2 How do I know if my business is profitable?

The Inland Revenue and, if your business is a company, the Registrar of Companies require you to draw up accounts, normally once a year, in accordance with certain rules and accepted practices. These accounts will tell you whether the business has made a profit in the accounting period.

But this information is not enough for management purposes as the information it contains is historical. You need to know whether your business is profitable at this moment and whether it will continue to be profitable and solvent in the future. You can only know this if accounts are regularly drawn up, preferably once a month. The purpose of these 'management accounts' is two-fold; firstly, to see whether your goods and services are selling at a profit and, secondly, whether you will have sufficient cash resources to meet your day-to-day liabilities.

You also need to set targets by preparing a budget: later on you can measure your performance against these target figures.

We discuss budgeting and management accounting in more detail in later chapters.

3 How do I know if I am doing well compared to other businesses?

When you run a business, only you can effectively decide if it is doing well. You cannot, as an employee will, compare your salary and benefits with other employees in the same job.

You can look at the accounts and compare them with companies in the same line of business, but the comparison can be complex and unreliable. Moreover partnerships' and sole traders' accounts are not available to the public. You can also compare the profit you earn from your share in the business with the amount you could have earned from alternative investments (e.g. interest on a building society account). But these financial comparisons ignore the intangible benefits of running your own business, for example, job satisfaction and the potential for future profits.

Professional advisers will give you an opinion on your business's performance and show you how to calculate some significant accounting ratios which will provide a yardstick from which you can judge your year-to-year performance. Some will provide surveys of your industry's performance. However, the most important comparison is between what you achieve and the targets you set yourself in your business plan.

4   Do I need to be an expert in all aspects of the business?   ●

Not unless you always intend to be a sole trader with no employees and even then you will often need financial and legal help. It is important to recognise your strengths and weaknesses and to know when you need help. A business uses a vast range of skills; marketing, financial, technical, personnel, legal, organisational among others.

There is no point in employing people and still trying to know as much about their job as they do. If you have the time and ability to know and do it all then you do not need the staff. It is a false economy to do everything yourself, if you could be more profitably occupied doing something else.

As the commercial world grows in complexity experts often have to refer to other experts or bring them into their organisation. You will need other people, as employees or external consultants, who will complement your own skills and abilities.

5   Do I need to be formal in running my business?   ●

Formality is very much in the eye of the beholder; some people are happier with a regimented approach, others prefer more flexibility. The law requires a formal approach to some record keeping (e.g. tax, VAT, PAYE), but otherwise formality is up to you.

The way you run your business must be compatible with efficiency and to some extent your own attitudes and those of your staff. There is little point in setting up detailed procedures if you are not going to keep up with them because you do not feel they are worth the effort.

However, informality is often a euphemism for lack of discipline. The owner who always prefers to trust his feelings rather than

13

collated data and considered planning is probably heading for bankruptcy. Few people have the inspiration to run a business profitably without some formality and even fewer external financiers will be prepared to rely on their instincts. If you do not like the paperwork you should employ someone else to do it.

● **6   Is my product a viable proposition?**

Before you commit financial resources to any product or service, take a good careful look and ask yourself – Is there a market for it? Who is my target market? It may seem like a novel idea but question why no one has done it before. If there is an existing market, who are your competitors and what percentage of that market can you hope to secure? Can your product or service stand up against its competition? What premises, equipment, workforce and capital would be needed in order to manufacture your product? Would you be able to recover your costs?

After conducting your market research, look at your projections – these should be over a two to three year period – do they indicate that the proposition will be profitable?

Secondly, consider all the possible consequences which could adversely influence your sale projections. Do not include any promises of future sales as these rarely materialise. Thirdly, does your product conform to any statutory safety regulations which may apply? And finally, does another company hold a patent for the product which you hope to manufacture?

Above all, know your market and apply the answers to these important, searching questions with knowledge and intuition gained from experience. If in doubt, seek out professional advice.

2 THE ENTREPRENEUR

7 What am I in business for?

If you do not know what your personal objectives are, you will probably end up dissatisfied with the progress of your business. It is also unlikely that your business will be a success if you do not give it direction.

Your first reaction may be that you are in business for the money. All but the most optimistic or foolhardy, however, will realise that, at least in the short-term, the personal financial gains of the owner may be small. The successful businessman is likely to want other rewards – independence, job satisfaction, security and an opportunity to use his own skills, for instance.

Your personal objectives and financial situation will influence the way you run your business. Be prepared to re-examine your objectives frequently as your needs will change. Only you can say what your objectives are at any time.

You should recognise that you may need to structure the future strategy of your business to meet your personal objectives. Thus strategic or corporate planning is an essential element in setting and evaluating your own direction. For example, a businessman may wish to attract external funds via the Unlisted Securities Market in order to capitalise on his past efforts and release finance for other, more personal, uses.

8 How do I motivate myself?

When you start a business, one thing is essential – enthusiasm. If you have no enthusiasm then there is little chance of motivating others into making your business successful – including your bank manager, employees and potential customers. But the practical problems of running a business, even successfully, can sap your personal enthusiasm.

If you cannot keep yourself motivated, you should probably be thinking of getting out of the business.

Keeping sight of your personal objectives will help. If the business is not helping you meet them, you may need to rethink the aims of the business or of your involvement in it.

It is common for the person who started the business to find it difficult to delegate. He can become bogged down in details and short-term problems and be unable to look ahead.

Recognise your own skills; the brilliant inventor is not necessarily equally good, or even adequate, as a manager or a salesman. But there are at least two options: delegate to others or learn new skills. The first option is difficult when the business is small and you may also fear that control is slipping away from you, but you must learn to stand back and rely on others. Learning is a good aim for most people as long as you do not try to do everything. You can learn from your professional advisers, employees, business associates: you may want to go on a training course. Think about how important it is for you to keep up-to-date with your original skills: you may find you enjoy other aspects of your work more.

Are you doing too much – or worrying about what you have not done? This can easily destroy your motivation. Attention to regular planning, setting priorities and allocating resources will help you decide what the solutions to your problems are.

● 9   Do I need to plan my own time?

The answer is yes as otherwise there is a danger of doing what you enjoy most or responding to the person who shouts loudest and most frequently.

Personal planning involves:
– deciding what you are going to do and how long it will take you;
– considering who will need how much of your time;
– working back from the deadline for each task and allocating periods of time for doing it before that date;
– liaising with others to make sure your plan fits in with theirs.

Do not leave out routine tasks when you draw up your personal plan: for example, seeing staff, planning for the long-term, answering correspondence and monitoring. If you do use this time for other tasks, reschedule as soon as possible. Take account of long-term as well as short-term tasks. It is easy to become absorbed in day-to-day problems and never to stand back to see where you are going.

Do be realistic, you cannot possibly find time to do everything. You also need an appropriate amount of leisure time, even though running a business will require willingness to work long hours.

10 How much time should I devote to personal planning?

The ultimate responsibility for the business is yours; you have to make sure not only that you do your own tasks but also that everyone else is doing theirs. There will be decisions that you alone can make. Therefore it is vital that your personal planning is as thorough as your business planning.

The time involved depends on the complexity of the business and the extent of your responsibilities. A good plan will save time for you and other people but do not be ruled by your original plan: no one can foresee what will happen and things will rarely go exactly as anticipated.

Do not have a planning procedure which is over-sophisticated. You will save time by starting simply – keeping a diary or a number of lists – and adding extra procedures and paperwork as you feel they are necessary.

As you become more experienced at planning and at estimating how long each job will take you, the time you devote to planning will be used more efficiently. Frequency of attention to planning will nearly always reduce the time it takes.

Remember to communicate your own plan to the people affected, so that they can plan accordingly.

11 Why is planning necessary?

Planning should ensure that:
– you work out your objectives;
– you determine the priorities;
– you do not forget essentials;
– you have enough resources available at the right time and in the right place;
– you do not take on too much;
– you can see how well you are doing at a later stage. If you do not have a target, you cannot judge your performance.

3 THE BUSINESS PLAN

12 Do I need a business plan?

Think of your business plan as a map which helps to show you the way to your destination. You decide where you are going but the map helps you to decide which route to take and assists you to stay on course during the journey. A map is essential if you have not made the journey before. Running a business involves making new journeys into unknown territory. There will be new factors affecting the business with constantly changing criteria which will make each year different. Thus a business plan is an essential business tool to help you to see clearly the way ahead.

Your business plan may be a simple statement of your intentions or an elaborate formal document depending on your purpose. But whatever the purpose the business plan should:

(a) state your business objectives;

(b) describe how you propose to achieve those objectives.

A business plan is a management discipline which provides you with a regular opportunity to stand back from day-to-day business matters and think about where your business is today and where you want it to go in the future. You will be able to assess the business environment in which you operate, the opportunities and threats it presents and the nature of the competition that you will face. This will help you to form your conception of the way in which your business will develop in the future. Out of this conception you will formulate objectives which initially will be qualitative but subsequently will require quantification. Thus your business plan is a quantitative and a qualitative statement of your business objectives and requirements over the next three to five years.

There are two important uses for your business plan:

– internal management;

– external fund raising.

The main purpose of your business plan is internal management planning and control. It is sound practice to involve key members of your management team in the preparation of the plan. This has two important benefits; firstly, their ideas and comments may prove useful to you and secondly, by involving them you are likely to gain a stronger commitment to your business plan from your staff. When you have produced a plan, it should be used as a management control document by which the actual performance of the business is measured on a regular (usually monthly) basis over the period covered by the plan. This regular comparison between business plan and actual performance can be structured in such a way that it enables you to monitor the business as a whole as well as each main management function (e.g. sales, production, etc.). This will assist you in analysing the causes and effects of any variations from the plan within your business. It will also help you to delegate responsibility for the activities of the business to members of your management team.

The second important reason for having a business plan is to assist you in raising additional funds externally. Your bank manager or other potential investors will require details of your plans for the future of your business. A well structured and formally documented business plan will assist you to present your business in a favourable manner.

● **13   What does a business plan contain?**

This will depend on the purpose you have in mind. There will be a considerable amount of quantitative information that you will want to show and this is best presented as schedules and charts included as appendices to the text. The text should describe your business plans for the future and specifically provide a concise but comprehensive interpretation of the business objectives as shown in numerical terms.

The structure of the plan may vary from one business to another but a typical format for a manufacturing business could be:
  (a) executive summary;
  (b) the business and its products;
  (c) marketing;
  (d) production;
  (e) research, design, distribution or other significant operations;

(f) management and personnel profile;

(g) financial analysis.

In addition, if the business plan is to be used as a part of a submission for raising finance, an extra section should be inserted preferably after the executive summary covering the history of the business.

The business plan should describe and quantify the business objectives in each main function of the company and explain how these will be achieved. It is essentially a practical document representing a management action programme. For instance, the marketing plan should describe the forecast developments in the market and the competitive forces in operation; it should also set clear objectives for product sales in each territory. These objectives should be detailed as a sales forecast in an appendix and can be translated into an action programme for each sales representative.

As part of the explanation of how objectives will be achieved, the business plan should detail the resources that the business will require. Thus the document should include plans for manpower, buildings, plant and equipment, working capital and funding. Each of these aspects will be dealt with in the appropriate section of the plan but a consolidated requirement for manpower and funds should be summarised in the appendices.

One of the most important items in the plan will be the statement of the overall financial performance of the business. The main financial statements should be presented for each year covered by the plan; these should comprise trading and profit/loss accounts, balance sheet and cash flow. In addition, other important figures and business ratios should be included as required; e.g. sales order book, overdue orders, stock turnover, capital expenditure, return on capital employed, profit/sales percentage, debtors ratio, etc.

14 How do I monitor performance against the plan?

You can monitor the actual performance of your business against the plan by using a management reporting system. It is important to ensure that both the business plan and the management report are structured in the same way so as to facilitate the comparison of information. The two should be designed together as part of the same system.

The preparation of the plan and report is best done by using a computerised planning and control system. There are many powerful microcomputer systems available on the market to help you to model your business plan through a series of 'what if' questions. The same system can be used to record and report actual business results and compare these against the plan to produce an analysis of variances. It can also be linked to your accounting and production control systems to enable a reliable flow of data from source to your reporting system. This will facilitate explanations of variances, for example, if your record of materials purchased exceeds the forecast in your plan, the system could trace the suppliers' invoices.

The monitoring of actual performance against the plan will involve a quantitative comparison of information. But it is also important to include a regular commentary on the performance of the business as part of the management report. Such a commentary would enable your managers to interpret the results, to explain variances in performance and to comment on future prospects. Moreover it provides them with the opportunity to report on their performance where they are accountable to you.

An important part of developing the management reporting system is to decide the frequency, content and format of reports. Regularity is essential when monitoring the performance of a business but too much data too often could make the exercise more time consuming than useful. You need to ensure that you divide your time effectively between planning, control and the other duties you have to perform in running your business.

You need to make a careful choice of schedule for the frequency of information reporting. Typically management information for decision-making is provided on a daily, weekly and monthly basis. Longer reporting periods, i.e. quarterly, half yearly and annually, would normally represent a consolidated summary of monthly results. You may decide that you need certain information on a daily basis, e.g. sales deliveries, cash takings and bank balance. Other information is necessary on a weekly basis, e.g. sales orders, production output. These are typical aspects of the business where fast corrective action may need to be taken if results differ from the plan. Most businesses use a monthly cycle of reporting for the main monitoring of business performance. A typical monthly report would include a full set of management accounts detailing, as appropriate, corporate, divisional and product profitability together with balance sheets, cash flow statements and projections, as well as other salient figures and business ratios. The monthly report provides a suitable agenda for a management meeting to monitor performance and to plan operations in order to ensure the continued achievement of business plan objectives or to review operations in the light of changed circumstances.

15 How often do I need to update the plan?

Generally a plan should be re-compiled each year. A typical business plan for small and medium-sized companies will cover three to five years into the future. The first year of the plan, often referred to as the budget, may be prepared in greater detail usually with more information about sales and costs, and broken down into monthly periods for the purpose of subsequent monitoring of performance. This allows you to show and take into account any seasonal peaks and troughs in your business. You can also flex your budgets (see question 18) to facilitate comparisons and improve your decision-taking. The subsequent years of the plan will usually cover a full operating period.

The annual planning process will involve rolling forward the 3 to 5 year plan by a year. This provides you with the opportunity to review the old plan against the actual performance and reflect upon any changed circumstances that affect your outlook for the future. Having considered the new scenario you are able to compile the detailed budget for the first year. It is good practice to prepare and publish the plan before the start of the new year.

This annual planning cycle is a major exercise and could mean that both yourself and your management team commit a great deal of time to it over a period of some weeks. In general, therefore, a business plan should stand without amendment for a year until the next planning exercise. However if business circumstances change dramatically it may be necessary to re-compile the plan. For example, you may wish to produce a new plan during the year as part of a presentation to raise external finance.

It is also good practice to allow the detailed budget to stand without amendment for the full year. If actual circumstances change then these can be reported as variances to the budget and explained as necessary with or without the use of the flexing procedure. However, occasionally an unforeseen event during the year fundamentally affects the validity of the budget, e.g. a division of the company is sold or a major product line is closed. In these circumstances you may prefer to compile a revised budget for the rest of the year.

It can also be useful to review the actual performance against the budget after six months and to prepare a revised forecast of the likely outcome for the full year. During the second six months you could monitor performance monthly against both the original budget and the updated forecast.

4 PLANNING AND MANAGING YOUR FINANCES

16 How do I know what profit I have made?

In order to measure your profit, you must monitor your performance. The best method of doing this is to produce management accounts regularly, probably on a monthly basis, and ensure that these accounts are available quickly. It is no use having them six months after the period in question if quick remedial action is possible – you will have lost six months' profit by then.

The information contained in your management accounts package will be determined by the nature of your business, but the following would normally be included in the profit and loss account:

Turnover – the invoiced amount of sales, analysed where appropriate by product, division or branch.

Gross Profit – the profit earned on those sales, after deducting the direct costs of manufacture or purchase. Precisely what costs are treated as direct will depend on the nature of the business, but the important point here will be to ensure that there is consistency of treatment.

Overheads – the recurring expenses of running the business, which normally do not vary significantly with the level of turnover.

Net Profit – this is the 'bottom line' and will tell you how much profit (or loss) has been made.

In addition to the profit and loss account referred to above, the management accounts package should include a balance sheet showing the assets and liabilities of the business.

17 How do I keep control of my finances on a day-to-day basis?

The monthly management accounts will give a good indication of trends, when you compare one month with another. It is also important to have a 'feel' for the performance of the business at all times. This can be achieved by monitoring the 'key' aspects of the business more frequently. Depending on the nature of the business, the key aspects might be:

Daily takings – this would be relevant in a retail shop or a restaurant or public house.

Order input – where there is a very quick cycle from receipt of order to delivery, and typically where order values do not fluctuate significantly, the level of new orders received is the best indication of future business.

Despatches – where invoicing is only done periodically, it may be necessary to monitor the volume of goods despatched in order to get an indication of the invoice value.

In a large organisation individual departments may have their own 'key figures'. If these are collected centrally the management can get a good pulse reading on the health of their business. However, these overviews are no substitute for the full accounts package which will provide a more precise analysis of the profitability of the business.

18 What do I do to measure my need for cash and working capital?

It is essential for every business to plan for its future development and every business plan must include budgets for future trading periods. There should also be projected balance sheets and detailed cash flow projections. These will give you an indication of your cash and working capital requirements.

Cash flow projections and projected balance sheets are necessarily subjective documents. They are derived in part from assumptions made about the trading prospects for future periods. If the trading forecasts are exceeded, or perhaps not achieved, it is likely that the cash flow projections will require modification. If turnover is higher than forecast, this should have the effect of enhancing profitability. In the short-term, however, when purchases have to be paid for and debtors are still outstanding, that increased turnover is likely to place pressure on the cash flows and result in increased borrowing requirements. The way to steer clear of the bankruptcy courts is to keep a balance between these inflows and outflows.

A 'flexed' budget whereby variable elements, e.g. turnover or cost of sales, are moved up or down can indicate the effect of such movements on cash flows, profit and working capital. If the sensitive variables and inter-relationships in the business are identified, it is relatively easy, manually or using a ready-made software package on a small computer, to flex a budget in this way.

The businessman who understands how his cash requirements fluctuate with different trading conditions is far more likely to be able to present to his bank manager or other sources of finance a case that will ensure he obtains any borrowing facilities which he requires. If he is fortunate enough not to need to borrow, he will also be better able to identify surplus cash and ensure that these funds are invested to earn interest.

The cash flow projection will include assumptions as to the timing of payments of debtors and creditors. There are essentially two types of factor which influence these payment patterns:

External factors – how much pressure do your creditors place on you for prompt payment? How resistant are your debtors to the pressures you place on them for prompt payment? These factors are not necessarily within your control.

Internal factors – these are within your control and can determine precisely when you make payments, and by efficient credit control, you can influence how quickly you receive payments from debtors.

It is important to realise the inter-relationships of these factors and to recognise how far you can go in influencing them. Once you have established payment patterns which your creditors will accept, you can calculate your cash requirements as part of the overall business plan, and by flexing your budget you can identify how your cash budget will be influenced by other changes in market forces. You can also calculate, by stretching your creditor payment pattern and by speeding up debtor collections, how you can respond to cash pressures.

It must be remembered, however, that cash flow projections only show requirements at one point in time – normally at the end of the month. Within the month requirements may vary significantly and the true peaks and troughs may not necessarily have been reflected in the cash flow. This is where regular monitoring is required to ensure that cash is managed on a daily basis, and that prior warning is received of any problems. Close monitoring will also help you to provide for large periodic payments – for instance, the quarterly VAT remittance – and will ensure that they do not come as a surprise, placing undue strain on the available cash resources.

● 19 What form should my cash budget take?

It is difficult to generalise on the form that a cash budget should take. It should be the form that is the most appropriate to your business.

Most accounting systems are designed to produce information to facilitate the preparation of financial accounts and the analyses and breakdowns they require. Cash flow budgeting may require further analysis which is not readily available from the cash book breakdowns. For example, if there is a 'Purchase Ledger' column in the cash book, it may be necessary to make manual adjustments to analyse these payments between goods and VAT for cash flow accounting.

The budget should be in the form that presents an analysis of receipts and payments that is useful to the management of the business. It should provide comparisons between budget and actual movements in the period under view together with cumulative figures for the financial year or half year under review. Explanations for significant variations should be provided. It is also important to compare the financing facilities available to the business with the funds in use.

As a business becomes more complex with expansion and diversification, it is important to bear in mind that the budget should only be a summary of the projected movements. If too much information is included, it becomes difficult to separate the important from the inconsequential. Brevity and succinctness are just as important in presenting financial figures as they are in the written word.

Cash budgets in isolation can also be dangerous if they are not viewed as part of the overall management information systems. For example, if the actual bank overdraft is £100,000 less than the budget this might be good news, but if the sole reason is that the last quarter's VAT liability of £200,000 has not been paid, a further comparison of the budget and actual balance sheets will reveal an ominous accumulation of liabilities.

The cash budget must therefore be treated as one aspect of the overall management information system, and the management must understand that the cash budget will be influenced by the business's ability to meet its trading projections generally.

20 Can I pay my creditors more slowly?

This depends on two factors:
− How quickly they are being paid at present.
− How long they are prepared to wait for payment.

We all like our customers to comply with our credit terms or to negotiate arrangements that are acceptable to both sides. Your suppliers would no doubt want you to do the same. If you are to react quickly to the business opportunities that arise, you are going to rely on the co-operation of your suppliers whose goodwill will have been earned from past trading relationships.

It is possible to take an extra couple of days' credit without damaging long-term relationships, but a deliberate policy of extending the credit terms on all occasions is likely to lead to strained dealings with suppliers, particularly where there are not a number of alternative suppliers all ready to accept your new business. If you are placed on 'stop' by suppliers for late or non-payment of their invoices, then it may disrupt your production cycle and cost more than the few days' interest you will have saved. Suppliers who recognise you as a habitual late payer are also likely to build the late payment interest into the prices they charge you.

It is best to consider payment terms as one aspect of the contract with your supplier, and negotiate the best overall deal you can get. If you commit yourself to meeting his payment terms, you may be able to negotiate a settlement discount, or alternatively, a lower price. If you commit yourself to purchase from a small number of suppliers, you may be able to negotiate bulk or loyalty discounts which may be more advantageous to you than extending the payment terms by a few days.

It is also important to appreciate that deferring payments can lead to the accumulation of large balances. When cash resources are tight and the business is operating at the limit of its facilities, these large balances can make you vulnerable. A number of those businesses who deferred payment of PAYE, NI and VAT during recent periods of Civil Service industrial disputes were subsequently forced out of business when the demands for payment eventually arrived.

Rather than taking extended credit when conditions are bad, consider first the possible side-effects mentioned above, and also the following alternatives:

– Improving cash flow by accelerating payments from your debtors through more effective credit control.

– Approaching major creditors and agreeing to revised payment terms, providing extended credit as part of an overall package.

– Seeing the bank manager and agreeing an increased cash facility. He should be receptive to a well-reasoned argument that the business's existing facility is inadequate, particularly if the projections for the business show increased profits, and the balance sheet shows that there is adequate security on which the lender can rely.

● **21   Is a pound today worth more than a pound tomorrow?**

All commodities have a price. Money has its price, and that price is interest. If you have to borrow money you pay the lender interest for the use of his money. If the money is yours, interest can be earned from investing it. This is very basic but it goes a long way towards answering the question.

If an economist were asked this question, he would start talking about the rate of inflation, the rate of interest and the 'real rate of return' which is the extent to which interest rates exceed the rate of inflation. In times of high inflation the prospect of repaying yesterday's borrowings in today's pounds is not so onerous. The domestic housing market in the early 1970s is a classic example of this; £5,000 borrowed to buy a house in 1970 would be easily repayable out of sale proceeds of, say, £10,000 two years later, but if you then needed to borrow £10,000 to buy a comparable house, how much have you really gained?

The problem of how to account for inflation has been a thorn in the side of the accountancy profession for a number of years, and the academic arguments still continue. What practical advice can we offer to the non-accountant in these circumstances? At the time of writing, inflation is running at approximately 5%, whereas bank base rates are 11.5%. Most businesses have to pay up to 3% over base rate for their borrowings. There is, therefore, a real cost to pay for borrowings.

The businessman can therefore conclude that early payment of creditors costs money whereas prompt receipt of debts saves money. Other considerations enter into this problem as we have already discussed, so that interest should not be the sole factor in your cash management decisions.

More difficult questions are raised by settlement discounts and instalment payments. For example:

– If bank borrowing is costing 15% per annum, does a 1% settlement discount for prompt payment within, say, 21 days of invoicing cost or save money?

– Is £90 received now better than four quarterly payments each of £25, when the cost of borrowing is 15%?

Dealing with the second question first, a discounted cash flow calculation would show that the deferred terms are marginally better. However, in looking at the problem practically, if a debtor is offering these terms you should also consider whether he will still be good for the instalments in three, six and nine months' time. If the risk factor is high, this might subjectively override the mathematics of a discounted cash flow calculation. Changes in interest rates will also influence the answer, and anyone who can accurately predict interest rate movements should be playing the money market rather than any other kind of business.

The first question is easy to solve mathematically once you know how quickly you will be receiving payment. At 15% per annum interest rate, if payment is accelerated by 24 days or more, you save money, if it is not, then you do not save money. Unfortunately, it is not as simple as the straightforward mathematics. If you offer a settlement discount for payment within a fixed number of days, what do you do if someone takes longer than that period to pay, but still takes the settlement discount? If you grin and bear it you are losing money. If you take issue with the customer you may well spend more time and expense in getting the balance than the amount at stake is worth. You may also damage your trading relationship with the customer. It is necessary to understand the mathematical aspects of the calculation, but you must also take into account the commercial considerations and form your view in that overall context. In particular, if you are looking at the prospect of money in the future, in the present climate of business failures, consider the credit risk. This is a subjective judgement and will lead cautious businessmen to accept the pound now, while the optimists will take the pound plus in the future.

5 FINANCING THE BUSINESS

● **22   How do I make a choice between investment options which will help develop my business?**

The most important step is to consider carefully what the objective of the business is. Is the aim to make as much profit as possible in a short space of time, to maximise profits in the long run, or to generate a large quantity of cash?

Once you have defined your objective, the principal determining factor is the potential return which the different investments are expected to produce. The most common methods of calculating returns are:

(a) The pay-back period which shows how long it will take for the investment to produce sufficient cash and profit to cover the original outlay;

(b) The return on capital employed. This figure is calculated using the annual profit divided by the cost of capital employed in the project. The true return on capital employed will vary with the nature of each investment opportunity. Some projects may require considerable working capital as well as the capital cost of the plant or equipment and this would need to be taken into account in determining the rate of return on the capital employed.

Actual cash flows may vary significantly from one project to another. Where there are several alternatives under consideration, it may also be helpful to discount all future cash flows to their estimated current values. Then you can compare them on a more meaningful basis (using internal rate of return and net present value techniques).

More important than the choice of method is an analysis of the margin of safety offered by each investment opportunity. Future returns will be estimates, so you need to see how sensitive the final outcome is to changes in forecast revenues or costs.

The nature of the investment or project chosen will also have a significant impact upon the current activity of the business. You need to consider whether the investment is compatible with current operations. Is it an extension of these operations, or would it represent a diversification? If it represents a new area, have you sufficient experience? Will your current staff be able to run the project and will management be able to control it? If not, then will it be possible to recruit new staff, and how will this recruitment affect the attitude of existing staff? Finally, you should consider whether the level of risk involved in the investment is similar to the risk of current activities. If not, then you should consider whether you wish to have a spread of risk, or whether you wish the business to be entirely high or low risk.

The tax implications of the possible investments also should be considered. Depending on the nature of the investment and its location, there may be varying levels of government grants or allowances available.

Certain investments may appear to offer an acceptable rate of return, but may have an unfortunate impact upon the reported results of the business. The purchase of premises provides a solid asset base in the balance sheet and is likely to attract a relatively low depreciation rate. In contrast, accepted accounting practice requires that the cost of purchased goodwill should be written off over a relatively short period. If it turns out that the profits generated by this goodwill arise over a longer period, then the reported return for the first few years will be lower than the real return.

Finally, the availability of finance may affect the choice of investment. If finance for it is to be obtained externally, then lenders may wish to be given security on the assets involved. Only certain types of assets can have such a charge attached to them. The type of investment must be compatible with the type of finance available, as discussed in question 24.

● **23 How do I know what I can afford to borrow?**

It is certainly not true to say that you should borrow as much as people are prepared to lend you – if only because this would be unnecessarily expensive. Your borrowing should be restricted to what you need. Will you be able to afford what you need?

You have to determine how you will repay your borrowing; both interest and capital repayments. In some cases, a lender may be prepared to give a capital repayment 'holiday' to allow the business to generate sufficient cash flow to repay the loan. Profit and cash flow forecasts will therefore be necessary to establish the repayment capacity of the business.

Two key indicators used by most lenders to decide whether someone can afford the loan they are requesting are capital gearing and interest gearing. The capital gearing of a business is expressed in the ratio of borrowed funds to equity funds. There is no ideal ratio, and ratios vary greatly depending on the nature of the business. As a rough guide, any lender is likely to review very carefully the safety of a proposed loan if it takes the ratio of loans to equity over the 1:1 level.

Interest gearing is the number of times the interest payments are covered by the expected return on the investment, e.g. if you borrow £100 for a year at 10% interest and expect to make £30 profit out of which the £10 interest will be paid, then the interest is covered three times. A useful standard is to ensure that interest payments are covered at least twice by the recurring profits of the business.

Your ability to borrow will also be determined by the amount of security that you or your business has to offer. This might be a fixed charge over the premises of the business, or a floating charge over the business assets. Any lender will take a conservative view of the value of the security and in most cases this calculation will be less than the cost shown in the balance sheet. Alternatively, the lender may require some form of personal guarantee supported, for example, by a charge over your own property.

24 Where do I go for finance?

This depends on the purpose for which the money is needed. For example, if the finance is to be used for a capital investment which will only generate returns in the long-term, then the finance should be repayable over a long period. On the other hand, if funds are required for a new venture involving a high degree of risk, then equity finance would probably be appropriate.

The principal sources of external finance can be split into two categories, debt funding and equity funding. Debt funding means that repayments will be made over an agreed period and the loan will usually be secured by the assets of the business or by personal guarantees. Bank overdrafts are usually used to finance the net working capital requirements of the business. The overdraft should 'turn over' on a regular basis; a bank may become concerned if there is a permanent hard core element in the overdraft. Other short-term facilities available from most UK and overseas banks include bonding facilities, export finance and discounted bills of exchange. The same banks together with such other institutions as Investors in Industry will also supply medium-term loans (between 2 and 10 years) mainly to finance specific projects. Longer-term debt funding (usually up to 20 or 25 years) is normally in the form of commercial mortgages on property or long-term loans again from institutions like Investors in Industry. Other forms of finance include hire purchase, leasing and debt factoring.

Equity capital may be forthcoming from a variety of sources and is often combined with some form of debt funding. The Business Expansion Scheme represents a good source of medium-term equity funding as it offers considerable tax advantages to investors. All the major banks have venture capital subsidiaries who may be willing to invest and there are many specialist venture capital companies. A useful reference book of venture capital companies is the *Sunday Telegraph Business Finance Directory*.

The most important consideration before you approach any lender or investor is to define clearly why you want the money and how it will be repaid. Your accountant will assist you in raising the necessary funds.

He will help you to establish your true requirements, assist you in preparing a concise business plan and financial forecasts and introduce you to a suitable lender or investor.

● 25 What information will investors expect from me?

Investors will expect enough information to enable them to make the initial investment decision and to assess the progress of the company with the benefit of the new funds.

The precise information required will depend upon the amount invested, the security available and the type of investor.

Generally a potential investor will want to see a business plan which sets out your assessment of the market place, your proposals for the business and how they relate to the market place, your own background and experience and your requirements. The business plan is a selling document which should be designed to persuade the investor that your business would be a worthwhile and profitable investment. The plan would have to be supported by realistic forecasts of the profits and cash flow of the business and the balance sheet position.

After the investment decision has been made, the investor may want to be kept informed of the company's progress. This should not be an onerous task and will probably entail a short report supported by regularly updated cash flow forecasts and the latest management accounts and prompt completion of statutory financial statements.

● 26 How do I demonstrate that I am credit-worthy?

The major evidence of credit-worthiness will be provided by your past record. A lender is likely to be favourably impressed if you can demonstrate a successful business record and, in particular, prompt repayment of previous loans.

The lender may also take into account the performance of previous businesses in which the owners or directors have been involved. The successful management of a personal bank account and orderly repayment of personal loans would also be a good indicator.

You can also demonstrate your likely future credit-worthiness by showing that you have planned properly for the future. If you are able to provide realistic profit and cash flow forecasts this is likely to help; particularly if you can show that you have a good past record in achieving forecasts. You should also make clear that you have taken every possible eventuality into account, such as the likely actions taken by competitors and changes in the requirements of your customers.

A third party may be willing to confirm that they believe you are credit-worthy. Banks are frequently requested to provide credit references, and they will happily oblige provided that your account has been run properly.

Finally, you may be able to persuade another business or person to write you a letter stating that they intend to support you financially should you be unable to meet your liabilities. Although this is not a guarantee, it may still act as a positive indicator to a potential lender.

27 How important is my credit-worthiness?

It is very important, because most businesses survive on credit. The withdrawal of credit by major suppliers or lenders is a common cause of business failure.

Lenders must have confidence in the ability and integrity of the management. They are much more likely to have this confidence if they are kept fully informed of any significant developments and are regularly shown the results of the business. Trade creditors normally finance a large proportion of a business's working capital requirements and you should ensure that they are paid regularly.

The credit-worthiness of your business is often assessed by a credit reference agency such as Trade Indemnity plc. You should keep them informed of any developments which may affect their assessment. Suppliers often refer to these agencies, your own bankers or existing suppliers before deciding upon the level of credit to extend to you.

6 KNOWING WHAT IT IS COSTING YOU

● **28 How do I measure the cost of my products or services?**

Each product or service costs you the sum of many expenses, not just the raw materials used or the wages of the employee. To make a profit your total revenue must exceed all the costs of the business; therefore, in order to run a business profitably, you should know what all your costs are.

Measuring your costs starts with recording them accurately. There are many types of cost collection and accounting systems, manual and computerised; your accountant will advise on how to set up and operate a system suited to your business. But whatever system you choose, it must have controls to ensure that all transactions are recorded accurately.

When you have accurate cost data, you can begin to identify costs of individual products or services; this will help you to determine whether your prices cover your costs.

There are a number of systems of analysing costs, e.g. by product or by department. You must decide for what purpose you need the analysis: whether it be for setting prices or for monitoring staff performance.

If you plan to rely on the analyses of your costs for decision-making, you must update them regularly, not just as a once a year exercise, particularly in times of changing prices.

● **29 Which of my products or services is making money?**

The expression 'making money' can have a number of meanings in a business context.

You may mean that the sales revenue exceeds the **variable costs** (costs that change when output changes) of making a product or providing a service. For example, wool usage would be a variable cost in a woollen garments manufacturing business. The difference between your selling price and the variable costs is known as the **contribution.**

Costs that do not change with volume of output are called **fixed costs**, and these include such items as rent, rates and professional fees. Given the appropriate capacity the rent for our woollen garments factory would not change whether you made 10,000 garments in it or just one.

You may use the expression 'making money' to mean that your sales revenue exceeds all costs of the business including a share of the fixed costs.

Both meanings described above can be useful to someone running a business. If you know what your total fixed costs are and you know the contribution the product makes, you can work out how many products you must sell to 'break-even'.

Example 1

A company has only one product – Product X:

	£
Selling price	10
Variable costs	6
Contribution	£4

The company's fixed costs are £4,000.
It must therefore sell $\frac{£4,000}{£4} = 1,000$ units

to break even. If it sells less than 1,000 units it will not be covering all its costs; if it sells more than 1,000 units, it makes a profit.

So if you know what your break-even sales target is, you can monitor your profitability by comparing actual sales with the target figure.

In practice, however, things are generally more complex, especially where more than one product is involved. In such circumstances when you are making short-term decisions, you should concentrate on the contribution each product or service makes. The amount of contribution will help you decide, for example, whether you should accept an order at less than your normal price.

Example 2

Product Y

	£
Normal selling price	100
Variable costs	80
Contribution	20
Share of fixed costs	15
Normal profit	£5

If a customer offers to buy a quantity of product Y at £90 each, instead of £100, and you have the spare manufacturing capacity, should you accept the order? The contribution would be £10 per unit (£90 – £80) but when you deducted £15 in fixed costs, you would appear to make a loss. But remember that fixed costs will be there whether or not you accept the extra order. Because the order will make a contribution, all other things being equal, you should accept it as you would be making money on it. But be warned: there are many pitfalls in the allocation and apportionment of fixed costs to specific products, services or activities, which might lead to bad decisions. We discuss in question 32 some of the problems of apportioning and allocating such costs to particular products.

Over the longer term you can change the level of fixed costs: e.g. factory rent and rates can be changed by closing down or moving to different premises. Comparing total costs (i.e. including a share of fixed costs) with total revenue; product by product, will help you to identify your weaker products. You can then consider whether you would lose more money in contribution from these products than you would save in fixed costs in the long-term by withdrawing them from the market.

30 If a product does not make money, should I stop producing it?

If you persevere with a product, even though it does not cover all its costs, your profits may still be higher than they would be without that product: this is where the product at least makes a contribution to your fixed costs (see question 29).

You should however be concerned about such a product and examine it in detail to see whether it could be made profitable.

First look at your pricing policy. Are you in a very price-conscious market or do your customers place more emphasis on quality, delivery time, etc.? Are your prices competitive? A price reduction may lead to a big increase in sales volume and contribution. Could you raise your prices gradually over a period of time, without losing customers? (Pricing is discussed in more detail in Chapter 7.)

Then consider all the costs you incur in making and selling your product. Can you use a different, less expensive raw material or control your material usage more closely? Have you compared your suppliers' prices with their competitors' prices recently? Look at your labour costs. Is time wasted by poor production planning or by using outdated machinery or methods? Could better training increase output or reduce the number of sub-standard items produced? Would sub-contracting part of the work save money?

Do your competitors appear to be able to supply the market profitably even though you cannot? They may have more resources which enable them to buy the most modern equipment or a well-known brand-name favoured by customers. If so, you may not be able to compete in the long-term. But your competitors may simply be better organised than you are.

Finally, do some crystal-ball gazing. Over the next few years, is demand for your product likely to increase or decrease? Is it likely to be replaced by more modern technology?

Recognising that a product will cost you money in the long-term, rather than make you money, and then scrapping it quickly will allow you to concentrate your resources on more promising products.

31 How do I know whether my costs are under control?

The collection of variable costs and the allocation and apportionment of fixed costs will not tell you whether you are operating efficiently. To achieve this objective you need to apply some form of measurement or comparison.

Even today too many firms rely solely on comparisons with previous results ignoring or overlooking the fact that current and past circumstances may be totally different. The type and precise measure you use will vary with the size and scale of your business. But in all cases you should identify the key items and put more effort into keeping these costs under tight control.

Building contractors, for example, will usually prepare an estimate of cost often as a basis of a tender document. This estimate can be subsequently used as a means of controlling actual costs. Alternatively, a clothing manufacturer may decide to use a standard costing system under which standards based on the actual amount of time, or raw materials normally required, can be calculated in advance for later comparison with actual usages and expenditures. Even professional firms find value in using this type of approach to the conduct of their work. In all cases, variances between actual and estimated or standard costs require explanation, identifying areas for management action in order to reduce costs and raise efficiency.

One advantage of a standard costs system is that it can be directly tied in with a firm's budgeting system; and it can be limited to provide detailed information about materials only, or alternatively, labour in a labour intensive operation. But in all cases the systems themselves only provide information to facilitate more meaningful decision-taking. They do not provide the answers.

● 32 Do I really need to allocate all overhead costs to products or departments?

Some costs are specific to particular activities or products and can be allocated accordingly. Other costs which are not specifically related to a particular product or department, e.g. accountancy fees, insurance, factory rates, must be handled in a different way.

It is possible by making certain assumptions and policy decisions, to apportion such costs: for example, the factory rates bill can be assigned to each department on a pro rata basis to the floor space it occupies. But there may not be an obviously appropriate method of apportioning other costs such as the Managing Director's salary.

The purpose of identifying costs with products, services or other activities is to obtain information on which you can base decisions. In practice, however, the assumptions made can become so arbitrary that the information produced is of little use, indeed it can be so misleading as to be positively dangerous. However, it is unlikely that a single method of apportioning costs will be found which serves all the needs of the business.

There are alternative ways of looking at costs. For example, you can calculate only the variable costs of each product and treat the shared overheads as a general burden to be met in total by the various contributions of all your products.

The main advantages of apportioning all overhead costs are that selling prices can be compared more easily with costs. In addition managers are reminded constantly of the need to cover all business costs.

The disadvantages are the problems of actually performing the apportionment and the potentially demotivating effects of assigning certain costs to managers over which they have no control.

33   How can I control overhead costs?

Overheads are costs that cannot be traced directly to your products, although some may vary directly with output. They include such diverse items as electricity, management salaries, motoring expenses and heating. You must measure your overheads accurately and control them carefully, because their effects on your profits can be substantial.

Your business plan should include a forecast of expenditure for each main category of overhead costs, broken down into monthly

43

planned expenditure. If you then analyse your actual expenditure in the same way, you can monitor your overheads and see where corrective action may be needed.

Try to adapt a questioning attitude to the costs you incur when you are drawing up your business plan. Do not accept that expenditure must necessarily be incurred in future because you have incurred it in the past. Are there more cost-effective administrative routines you could adopt? Do you need all your factory space? Could you buy in services more cheaply than employing your own staff?

Think about how your overheads are incurred. Electricity that drives machinery will vary with machine usage and therefore with output; factory heating varies with the number of hours the factory is open; other items – management salaries, professional fees, rent – are related to policy decisions about the way the company operates and the facilities and services it requires.

You need to know what your overheads are and how they are incurred in order to identify ways in which they could be reduced and profits increased.

In addition, there are a number of management techniques which you may find helpful in applying a questioning attitude on a systematic, regular and thorough basis, whether you are concerned about administration, distribution, research and development, or sales and marketing.

● 34   How do I measure the cost of my stocks?

Many businesses have a large amount of their assets tied up in the form of stock – raw materials, work-in-progress and finished goods. In order to prepare meaningful management accounts as well as your annual accounts, you must put a value on your stock; but you must, for the sake of your profits, also know throughout the accounting period how much your stock has cost and what it is worth.

You need this information regularly so that you can cost your products accurately and also control the levels of stock – too much stock is an expensive luxury in warehousing costs and interest charges on the cash tied up.

The ease and accuracy with which you can measure the cost of your stock depends on many factors: e.g. the number of stock lines carried, the complexities of the production process, the nature and type of production overheads, the frequency of suppliers' price changes. You must, of course, keep accurate records of deliveries, prices and issues of stock in order to measure the cost (see question 63).

But various accountancy conventions have been developed to help you estimate the cost and value of your stock without the necessity of identifying each item separately. For this purpose, the cost of stock can be split into three parts:

Raw Materials

Similar items of raw materials will usually be stored together and it may be impossible to establish which consignment the items in stock were from. To resolve this problem, you can make an assumption about the sequence in which the items have been used.

FIFO – 'First-in, First-out' – is probably the most useful assumption for most businesses. You assume that when an order is received, from the production department or a customer, the oldest item is issued and therefore the items remaining in stock are the most recent deliveries.

Alternatively you can assume LIFO – 'Last-in, First-out'. You assume that the storekeeper always issues stock from the most recent delivery and therefore the stock items held in the warehouse are from the oldest deliveries. LIFO is not used frequently.

You can value stocks at a weighted average of previous prices; or forecast a price for the next few months – this is known as a 'standard' price. The assumption you choose to make will depend on the nature of your business.

Labour Values

Part of your total stock may be work-in-progress, that is, materials brought from others on which some work has been performed, but not yet complete. A portion of the cost of the partly completed product is the wages that have been paid for the work so far performed. So this labour cost should be included in the value of work-in-progress.

Other Costs

Accountancy rules allow only production overheads to be included in stock values (not administrative and selling/distribution overheads). Usually the average production overhead per unit would be included in the valuation.

As the value of your stocks will affect the reported profits of your business and the tax you pay, the valuation methods you choose are important. Accountancy rules state that normally you should keep the same method of stock valuation from year-to-year, so you cannot change simply to alter the reported profits of your business.

7 PRICING AND DISCOUNTS

35 How do I calculate my prices?

There are two ways to determine the selling price of your products
or services. They are:

(a) **The cost plus profit method.** Calculate how much labour and
materials will cost and then add the proportion of overhead costs
(e.g. rent, rates, depreciation, salaries, etc.) to be shared by that
product at the expected volume of business. To this total cost you
need to add a mark-up to cover your expected profit margin. The
total will suggest a selling price. (The problems of determining cost
are discussed in Chapter 6.)

(b) **The market price method.** You determine the market price
by studying the prices of similar products available from suppliers'
price lists, catalogues, advertisements or in the shops.

In practice the second method is dominant, as market forces will
tend to act to ensure that a competitive price is maintained; people
will not normally buy your product if they can obtain better value
elsewhere. Consequently, whatever price you have calculated using
the cost plus profit method, you will be unable to charge a significantly higher price than your competitors for the same item.

However you should use the cost plus profit method to compare
your prices against those of your competitors before you issue a new
price list or introduce a new product or modifications to an existing
product. This comparison is vital as it will help you to decide
whether you can sustain an acceptable profit margin on each product sold at market prices or whether you should abandon any
product or proposed new line of business (see question 6).

Before you take any major decisions it is always helpful to put
yourself in your customers' shoes. In practice, price is only one
competitive factor involved in a buying decision. Your potential
customer will also consider quality of design and manufacture,

delivery date, reliability of service, guarantee period, credit facilities and so on. Some of these factors may be more critical to him than others, indeed some may have important cost implications for him. Having considered these factors, together with the quoted selling price, he will buy where he perceives the overall best value to be at that time.

So, a simple comparison of competitors' prices with your own is not the full story. You should examine the perceptible features of your product or service relative to the competition and attempt to value these various factors to obtain a better assessment of comparative prices. Using this detailed product and price information and having your own cost structure to hand, you will be able to judge the best price for your product in order to achieve the desired volume of business at maximum profit margins.

● 36   Does the type of business I am in affect my price-setting?

The approach taken to calculate prices will vary according to the type of business. If you are manufacturing or trading in standard products then there is unlikely to be much room for manoeuvre from the present competitive price in operation in the market. You will need to match your competitors' prices and ensure that there is sufficient profit margin available for you at the volume of business you expect to achieve.

If your business provides a service you should use the cost plus profit method to calculate the basis of your price quote. You need to estimate the materials and direct labour hours required to provide the service. You may price the job by adding the overheads and profit mark-up to the materials and direct labour costs. Alternatively, you could calculate an inclusive hourly labour rate comprising direct labour, overheads and profit which is based on an anticipated level of chargeable hours. You may also wish to set a minimum charge on small jobs to avoid making a loss.

If you are in business as a sub-contractor then it is likely that you will be tendering for contracts to supply goods and services to government departments, local authorities or large companies. In this case you should prepare your bid using the cost plus profit method. Special care should be taken when preparing estimates for such contracts, as you may be vulnerable to the actions of your customers' staff or other sub-contractors. Delays, strikes and poor quality work on their part could significantly affect your performance. A reasonable contingency would be a prudent item to include in your quote. Finally, familiarise yourself with the rules and procedures covering such contracts. Government agencies and some large companies have special arrangements which must be followed.

37 Should I offer discounts?

Discounts reduce prices and hence gives away money. No businessman wants to be so cavalier unless he can see the return. The effect of discounting a published or list price is a lower net selling price; consequently the criteria for applying a discount are merely extensions of those for setting the original price. We have seen that each potential customer will perceive the best value offered to him from several factors including price. Moreover, different customers will assess selling factors with varying degrees of importance according to their needs.

Discounting is a selling tool which gives you scope for selective price cutting either to certain customers or in particular situations, for instance, where large quantities are traded or clearance of old stock is required. Where discounts are given they should only be at a level sufficient to clinch the sale. The commercial judgement and experience of yourself and your sales staff will determine how much discount you offer.

You should guard against discounting becoming an established standard practice in your business. Do not make it too easy for your sales staff to reach sales targets simply by allowing them to offer large discounts without regard to the profitability of each deal.

Price cutting can be a dangerous practice in which someone, generally the suppliers with the least financial resource, will be the loser. There have been many trade price wars in recent years resulting in a number of fatalities on each occasion. Sometimes these fatalities are large well-known companies; more often they are the small or medium-sized businesses which do not make the headlines.

By all means offer discounts to your customers but take care to whom and how much; above all make sure there are profits to be made in the long-term.

● **38 What form of discount should I offer?**

There are several forms of discount which you can offer.

(a) **Trade discount.** There may be a tradition or practice in your line of business to offer a discount to trade customers, wholesalers and other intermediaries. The level of discount can vary considerably according to the type of business. Discount levels can even vary in a given trade according to circumstances and you should use discretion to differentiate between your regular customers whom you wish to retain and the casual buyer who is making a one-off purchase.

(b) **Special discount.** Occasionally you will face circumstances which will require a different approach to pricing. You may be opening a new shop, launching a new product, or moving into a different market. Each of these may require special discounted prices to act as opening offers in order to attract new customers and establish your place in the market. Alternatively, you may have old or slow moving stock which you need to sell off quickly, so a discount would be appropriate.

(c) **Quantity discount.** If you are able to sell a large volume of your product to a customer who might be swayed by an offer of a higher discount, then you would do so with the knowledge that you will incur lower costs, such as cheaper materials because you can purchase at bulk prices, longer production runs, better utilisation of transport and possibly less administration. It is standard practice in some industries to publish a differential price list based on quantity ordered. Alternatively a quota system can be used which is effectively a retrospective quantity discount. An annual trading quota is set and if this is achieved by the end of the year, an agreed predetermined discount is applied to the full year's sales and a credit note or refund is issued to the customer.

(d) **Cash discount.** You may wish to provide an incentive to your customers to pay you early or even immediately. This discount reflects the saving in capital (interest) resulting from your better cash flow position. Depending on the relative cash flow positions of you and your customer, it can be worthwhile negotiating a discounted price for an immediate cash sale. If credit sales are made it may be advantageous to offer a predetermined discount for payment earlier than the standard credit terms.

39   How do I know if my prices are correct?

You may never know if your prices are correct because pricing is not an exact science. There are too many other technical, commercial and psychological factors involved in making a sale to be certain that the price is right. But an attempt should be made to ensure that your pricing structure enables you to achieve maximum profit objectives.

Assuming you have followed the advice given in answer to the previous questions and applied good commercial judgement and common sense when negotiating with customers, then you have made a good start in setting correct prices. But you will want to maintain confidence that your prices remain competitive.

There are several ways of monitoring your prices to ensure they remain at the correct level. In a competitive market any movement in your market share may indicate that your product has become incorrectly priced relative to your competitors' prices. This may be because one or more of your competitors has taken price action and therefore you will need to judge whether to respond immediately or to sit tight and closely watch customer reaction.

You should also regularly monitor any customer movement. If you are gaining or losing customers this may indicate that your prices are no longer correct. In fact, if you ask a customer why he is taking his trade elsewhere, he will probably tell you if it is due to your prices. Of course, your customers will readily and regularly tell you that your prices are too high, occasionally you can take them seriously especially when their orders start to decline.

You should develop a system whereby you can continually compare your prices with those of similar products or services on the market. This exercise should reflect the intangible factors such as delivery and guarantee period as well as any differential features between your product and that of your competitor. All these factors need to be assessed and valued in order to adjust prices onto a comparative basis. This monitoring procedure represents a considerable arithmetic exercise which is best achieved by using a simple microcomputer system.

8 SELLING AND MARKETING

● **40   What is marketing?**

The key to a successful business is marketing. Marketing is not just about selling. Its definition is broader, involving an understanding of your market and of your customers' requirements. Marketing helps you deliver your products or services to the full satisfaction of your customers; if you do not satisfy them, you do not have a business. It is therefore vital that every member of your staff is involved with marketing in the widest sense. In order to attract customers and ensure that they are fully satisfied you need to understand what they want and what makes them buy. It follows that the main marketing tool that you have is information.

● **41   How do I measure the size of my market?**

When you have established which market you are competing in, the first step is to measure the size of that market, the competitive forces at play within it and the factors affecting change. You will need to find out as much about the market as possible; one of the most important requirements is to know the number of your competitors and their market share compared to your own. It is also essential to understand the seasonal and cyclical market fluctuations. You should find out about the main customers in the market, the type of people they are, where they are located and take account of any source of dissatisfaction. Obtain a thorough understanding of the products already in the market, the uses to which they are put and the way that distribution is carried out. On a broader scale, get to know the political, economic and social environment affecting your market place, and any relevant legislation.

The broad term used to describe this analysis and understanding of the market is 'market research' of which there are three basic sources for obtaining information.

(a) **Existing research.** Large quantities of marketing information is already available to those businessmen who take the time and trouble to look for it. There are many sources of marketing information from organisations (e.g. The Market Research Association and the Industrial Market Research Society), trade associations, industrial research associations, universities and libraries. Information is available from government sources, particularly the Department of Trade and Industry and, for statistical information, Her Majesty's Stationery Office. Moreover there are many commercial sources of marketing data, including directories published by research associations and a plethora of market research organisations, often specialising in particular industries. Information can be gleaned from the banks, the newspapers, the Stock Exchange, stockbrokers, chambers of commerce, and foreign embassies. It is possible to take out a subscription with some of these organisations to ensure that you are regularly provided with the latest information on changes in your market.

(b) **Original market research.** If you require more specific data than you can find from studying existing market research you will need to commission an agency to carry out some relevant original research (you can obtain a list of market research agencies from the Market Research Association). Alternatively you can carry out some primary research of your own. Original research will usually involve conducting a survey among your customers, or a selected sample of the public at large. Care should be taken in the design and structure of the questionnaire and the phrasing of individual questions. There are several methods of obtaining information, through personal or telephone interviews, postal questionnaires, or even group discussions. When you have obtained the primary information, it is most important to ensure that it is analysed in a meaningful way and that the correct conclusions are drawn from the data.

(c) **Your own industry knowledge.** However much market research you carry out it should always be supplemented by your own intuitive knowledge and experience of the industry and market place in which you operate. Your customers provide a valuable source of information on the current state of the market, so make sure that you keep close to them and listen to their opinions and their requirements. A further prime source of data is your own internal information, such as sales enquiries, orders and deliveries and stock figures.

● 42 How do I find out what my customers want?

We have discussed in the previous question how we measure the size of the market; assessing intangible forces affecting the market, the likes and dislikes of customers etc. is known as qualitative market research.

Your customers will have desires and preferences in design, performance, reliability and so on and you will need to ascertain how your customers perceive your image compared to your competitors'. It is a less well-documented aspect of market research than the quantitative side mentioned in the previous question. However the three sources of information are the same. You can interpret statistics about customers' preferences up to a point, for instance the popularity of products according to their colour, shape, size, type, etc. Perhaps the most important source of information is from your customers themselves; you should keep in close contact with them and discover in general conversation their preferences and likes and dislikes, and particularly their opinions about your products and how you could improve them or give better value. It is important to listen to what they say and not believe they are saying something that you want them to say. Your prime objective is to satisfy your customer and you should remember that your product or service is not an end in itself, but a means of solving your customers' problems. The better you understand the customers' problems, the better products or services you will provide.

Another part of giving customer satisfaction is providing a service; even if you are only selling a simple product. All customers wish to receive service in a satisfactory and reliable manner. If you are providing a simple standard product then it is important to make that product different, indeed unique, through the service you provide. A typical slogan used by a service conscious business is *If you like our service, please tell others, if you don't then tell us;* this statement is an invaluable principle.

Market research is a continuous process; once you have found out what your customers like, you must keep up to date with their preferences and, as technology changes, ensure that you meet customer needs. For some products this will involve an overt change in the product presentation; for instance, the latest version of a microcomputer must incorporate and be seen to incorporate the latest technology. Alternatively some products, such as washing powders, achieve customer satisfaction through maintaining the same well-proven presentation whilst covertly undergoing several technological and quality changes over the years. These improvements ensure that customers' demands are met and maintained.

The key to market research is to find out what you can sell, and to make only what you can sell – not to try to sell what you can make. To measure how effective you have been in finding out what your customers like and how satisfied they are with your service, apply the following maxim: *Successful business is selling goods that do not come back to customers who do.*

43 How should I compile my marketing plans?

Many businessmen use the marketing plan as the first stage in the business planning process to define the market and to set sales forecasts for the business. It is not until forecasts of sales volume are set that the other functions of the business such as production, distribution and finance can commence their planning process.

The marketing plan is essentially a practical document which will describe the present position of the market and your business within the market place, stating your business objectives and describing how you propose to achieve those objectives. A major source of information for the preparation of the marketing plan is the qualitative and quantitative market research that you have carried out in assessing the size of the market and determining what your customers' likes and dislikes are. You will also need to assess your own past performance and your existing resources in setting the objectives for future trading. In describing the size of the market and the share of that market which you hope to achieve, you also need to decide which segments or 'slices' of the market you are going to approach, e.g. adults, children, professional people, retail, wholesale, private sector or the public sector; each of these will have an effect on the way you organise the resources in your business.

Having set sales forecasts for the volume and value of sales within the company you should analyse these into regions and territories; this will act as a target or sales objective for each of your sales personnel.

When preparing your marketing plan a useful principle to follow is the one known as Pareto's Law, which states that 20% of effort accounts for 80% of the total result, better known as the 80/20 syndrome. It has many applications within your business, but perhaps the most important is in marketing. Firstly, it is important that your risk is spread and that your business does not rely on a small section of the market. Secondly, make sure that you concentrate your efforts and spread your resources to cover those areas of your business where the greatest return is going to be achieved.

● **44 How do I advertise and promote my products and services?**

Advertisements have to be specifically targeted to generate active response. They must also stand out, identify the name of your product and the name of your business and provide the promise of a benefit to your customer, whilst also being consistent with the image of your business and your other forms of promotion. To achieve these objectives, advertisements should be of high quality and the preparation and the production of artwork and display material should be professionally produced. It is usually worthwhile to ask an advertising agency to carry out the creative work and then follow through with the design and production of the advertisement. Advertising agencies are also specialists in targeting the right markets and in the operation of media schedules: they will normally be able to book advertising space for you at economical rates. A list of suitable professional advertising agencies can be obtained from the Institute of Practitioners in Advertising (IPA).

There are many types of media and your choice will depend on the type of business and product you are marketing. There are newspapers – national, regional and local – local directories and Yellow Pages, trade magazines, consumer magazines, local radio, cinema, television, mail shots, posters and transport advertising, as well as the product's packaging and point of sale display material. You will need to compile carefully a strategy for presenting your advertisements in the media chosen; it is also most important that you have a method of measuring effectiveness of each type of advertising that your operate.

As part of your overall marketing strategy you will need to supplement your advertising with sales promotions. This may involve incentives, competitions, free offers and discounts to the trade, free samples and demonstrations and also discounts and promotional offers to the consumer. Other useful forms of promotional activities are demonstrations and stands at exhibitions. The Department of Trade and Industry issue an exhibitions calendar and the British Overseas Trade Board offers a similar service for international exhibitions.

Sponsorship is another form of sales promotion which can involve local sports, arts, management competitions and joint ventures with other companies offering complementary products in a non-competitive environment.

Perhaps one of the best forms of sales promotion is the use of editorial coverage in trade magazines, the local press or even the national press. Articles may be written for trade magazines based on new products or particular achievements; in fact, success stories generally receive positive and supportive response from the press. If we sometimes get the impression that only bad news makes good newspaper copy then perhaps it is because businessmen are slow to communicate their successes to journalists.

45 How do I organise my selling activity? ●

It is not possible to answer this question in detail as your selling resources will depend on the size and structure of your market. It is important to define your market and to divide it up into suitable territories; these will be based on the number of actual and potential customers in any geographical area. Another factor to consider is the number of accounts which a sales representative can handle successfully, this will depend upon your type of business and the products which you are selling. It is also probable that you will want your most important customers and key accounts to be looked after by senior staff, or, indeed, yourself.

Again, depending on the type of business, your selling activity may be organised outside the company by using wholesalers or distributors to arrange your local sales activity. Alternatively, agents can be appointed in certain territorial areas, a useful way of opening up in a new geographical region, particularly overseas. Another method of organising selling activity, which is becoming popular, is franchising. Basically you sell the rights to market your product or service in a certain area; this involves the franchisee's own capital so that he shares in both the risk and the reward.

It is important that you establish procedures and standards of performance for the operation of the sales force. You should ensure that your sales force carry out a programme of visits to customers in three categories: cold calling, prepared calling on both new and existing customers and repeat calls.

The balance must be maintained between these three types of visits and you should ensure that the prepared calls are sufficient to generate the required business. Depending on the type of business, cold calls will normally be in the minority. Make sure that your sales force plan the customer calls in advance, preferably by appointment, that they keep a record of appointments and that a full report is made each time a customer is visited. It is through such call reports that you will build up a data base on each of your customers, including detailed information about the company and its organisation as well as its buying habits and requirements. Make sure that you also keep proper records of sales inquiries, quotations sent and orders received. Document the reasons for lost orders and whether or not you may be able to recapture this business at a later date.

Finally, remember that your sales force are the ambassadors for your business; they are the people who meet the customer and they will influence whether your customer buys from you or your competitor. Your sales force should be properly trained so that your customers receive the highest quality of representation. Training should include:

(a) **Product knowledge.** This ensures that each sales representative knows what he is talking about and can accurately show how your product will work for the benefit of the customer.

(b) **Selling techniques.** This should cover how to carry out a sales interview, including identifying the customers' requirements, making the presentation, using promotional aids and closing the sale. It should also deal with the broader aspects of the characteristics of the market place and the industries to which you are selling, how it is organised and how buying takes place.

Remember also that communication is a vital part of your selling activity. It can be a lonely existence as a sales representative out in the field; he needs to feel that he is kept properly informed and motivated and you will need to ensure that your sales message is reaching your customer in a clear and positive manner.

In general, salesmen will also perform better if an incentive, through an individual bonus scheme, is in operation.

● 46 How do I monitor performance against my sales plan?

Your marketing plan will include a sales forecast analysed by territory so that each sales representative can be held accountable for his performance. The sales forecasts for each territory will be analysed by product and type of business and will include the sales volume, sales value and the gross margin and profit for each area. Each sales forecast can be used as a target for the individual salesman; this will be useful in motivating the salesman and acting as a budget with which to compare actual performance.

You need a sales accounting and reporting system designed in line with the sales forecast, so that the sales made by each representative are properly recorded and analysed by product and market segment so that both useful comparisons can be made and individuals' performances can be monitored.

You will then have both the actual and the forecast figures available so that variances can be reported to the sales management and representatives. It is important that regular weekly and monthly reporting takes place in case early corrective action is required. In this way sales reporting acts as a useful basis for discussion on the performance of individual sales representatives and as a basis for planning and re-forecasting the sales plans, in the light of changed circumstances.

47 How do I decide if an order is going to be profitable?

The overall sales reporting system must be capable of measuring the sales revenue from products against their respective costs. But, whilst it is important to calculate the actual profit according to the cost incurred on each sales delivery, it is perhaps more important to be able to forecast the expected profit on an order as it is received.

To determine the profit on a sales order, it is necessary to anticipate the costs that will be incurred in satisfying that sales order. The best way of achieving this is by setting a standard cost for each one of your products or services. There are, of course, many other good financial control reasons why you should have a standard costing system as part of your budgetary control procedures.

As sales orders are received you can measure the sales value against the standard product cost and calculate a standard gross margin. A system of reporting gross margin, analysed by product, customer, territory and market segment should be instituted and reports should be issued to management and sales representatives regularly. This early guidance concerning the profitability of sales orders is helpful in taking decisions on re-pricing or looking at costs of certain products where gross margins are seen to be out of line with that expected. It is also a useful way for you to compare the relative profitability of products sold to different customers and by different sales representatives.

Sales profitability reports can be used to gauge how close your standard product costs are to actual costs and to adjust your standard if necessary.

● 48   Where can I find new products or services to sell?

It is often said that if you have not got a new product to sell then you have not got a business. You cannot continue to rely on your old faithful products to keep your business going year after year; all products have their life cycles and you must appreciate that at some stage each of yours will reach its retirement. However, there is a considerable amount of product enhancement that you can carry out to extend the life of your existing products successfully.

The most usual way of extending the life of a product is to add more variations to the existing standard formula. You can also improve the quality or extend the features or perhaps make it more durable or more compact. Add extra convenience features to the product or find new uses for old products. Alternatively, you could leave a product as it is, but improve the delivery or the service or just enhance the packaging, making it more modern, more protective or more useful. Packaging may also be used effectively in a sales display. It is important that you monitor the life cycle of each of your products to ensure that you are able to anticipate well in advance the need for product enhancement and improve the product in time for the requirements of the market place.

However well you are able to enhance products and extend their life, it will always be necessary for you to be looking for new products and ideas to add to your product range. Again, many of your ideas will arise from the market research work that you should be carrying out on a continual basis. You will receive many ideas through your salesmen's reports from customers as to how they use your products and how they might be improved or developed, including omissions in your product range. You should also continually monitor your competitors' products and use good ideas to aid your own new product development. You can, of course, carry out your own technical research and development programme but this tends to be expensive and is a risk for which you may not receive an adequate return. It is better to use the research facilities available at universities, research organisations, and specialist consultancies.

You need to approach the development of new products very carefully. It is important to monitor the development of products and carry out proper market tests to ensure that you are producing a profitable product. Your choice of a new product will be achieved by a continual series of evaluations and investigations. Throughout the period of investigation, analysis and development you should remember that market requirements are the primary consideration in introducing a new product. Finally, ensure that the market has been fully tested and results properly analysed before a full scale launch is attempted. Remember, when you are planning to diversify into new products, to keep them related to your existing product base and make use of the existing sales, marketing, and distribution resources. An alternative method of diversifying is by acquiring another business with complementary products or services to your own.

49 What about exporting?

You may never have exported your products or services before, but there are plenty of people to help you with the procedures and documentation involved. In any case, you will probably find exporting is a healthy challenge and a source of profitable business. Many small and medium-sized businesses complement their domestic market by successfully competing overseas. However, it is necessary for you to do your homework and make use of the many forms of assistance that are available to you.

Your task is to determine the potential overseas markets for your products and services, select the key markets in which you will operate, then concentrate on developing them. You need to obtain market intelligence and information about the countries in which you hope to operate. Many factors beyond the nature of your product will influence you, including political, social, economic, and cultural differences between your domestic market place and that overseas. This will add a new dimension to your market research activities, but there are many organisations able to give you advice and information, particularly the exporting arm of the Department of Trade and Industry, the British Overseas Trade Board (BOTB).

Your market research will need to be carried out in a similar way to that already described for the domestic market. The BOTB will be able to provide much of the information about markets, their size and the different types of customers. The embassies of foreign countries will also be able to give you market intelligence, including the key users of products and services, potential agents and distribution sources. Other sources of information regarding export markets are from libraries, particularly the City Business Library in London, the *Financial Times* special market surveys, statistics produced by Her Majesty's Stationery Office and trade associations, and the international divisions of the major high street banks.

When you have assessed the market, you need to decide how to carry out your selling activity. You have the option of servicing your overseas customers direct or by using a distributor or agent. Be selective in the choice of distributors or agents in overseas countries. Normally they would have previous experience in their own territory, but it is important that they obtain good technical knowledge of your products and be able to make some decisions should a problem arise. You must have confidence that they can promote your products in a positive and profitable manner. Do not use an agent who is also selling for your competitors.

You may prefer to choose your own export sales representatives from UK personnel, but whilst it may be easier to train such sales representatives in the technical product knowledge necessary, it will be more difficult for them to appreciate the details of the overseas market and it may take several trips before they are fully acquainted with the peculiarities of each country, its market and each customer.

The financial aspects of exporting are also important. You should ensure that you take out credit insurance cover on export sales. This is available from both commercial sources and also from the Export Credits Guarantee Department of the Department of Trade and Industry. Commercial loans are also available from the banks to cover export contracts. Both the banks and the ECGD will be able to provide you with assistance in the exporting formalities and documentary procedures concerning the financing of export sales. You must follow the procedures strictly to ensure that you receive payment on time and in entirety.

9 BILLING CUSTOMERS AND COLLECTING MONEY

50   How can I collect my money more quickly?

The quick and easy answer is to make cash sales whenever possible or better still insist on cash with order even if only a deposit, with the balance due on delivery. In a society now dominated by borrowing and extended credit this may seem a somewhat old fashioned idea but there are some circumstances which allow for cash 'up-front', so take advantage of this most effective method when the opportunities arise.

However, we have become accustomed to selling on credit and without credit facilities industrial and commercial activity would not have developed at the rate it has. In short, credit facilities create sales opportunities. The granting of credit demonstrates your trust in the customer, but it can prove a very time consuming and expensive operation for your business, so it is most important to develop and operate a policy of strict credit control and fast and efficient collection of debts.

Your credit policy should define your terms of sale and the methods and procedures to be used in both accounting for and the assessment and control of credit accounts including the collection of debts. It is important to publish your standard credit terms as part of the conditions of sale on sales literature and the sales order acknowledgement, invoice and statement of account. You should negotiate and agree any variation from standard credit terms with the customer prior to sale, in order to avoid subsequent dispute and delayed payment. Also, read the small print on your prospective customer's purchase order and beware the inclusion of extended payment terms as a condition of trading. Take legal advice if you are in doubt.

Another method of collecting cash more quickly is to offer a cash discount incentive to your customer for payment by a certain date,

63

typically within seven or fourteen days from date of invoice. To offset the cost of the discount given you have the benefit of extra cash flow from, say, day 7 until perhaps day 60 or 90, when you would normally receive payment. Before offering a cash discount calculate the benefit to you of having cash in the bank earlier using your present cost of capital (e.g. your bank overdraft interest rate) and ensure the discount does not cost you more than the bank interest saved. An intangible benefit of this arrangement is the saving in credit management and collection costs, but to compensate for this you will find some customers accidentally or deliberately abuse the procedure and take the discount irrespective of payment date.

The basis of credit is trust, so be selective.

● 51 Can I improve my credit control system?

The basis of good credit control and fast and effective cash collection is a reliable and up-to-date sales accounting system. Make sure that invoices are despatched to the customer as quickly as possible. If your customer operates a monthly payment procedure, a one day delay in the despatch of the invoice could result in a one month delay in payment. A periodic statement of account, preferably monthly, detailing the current indebtedness should also be despatched as quickly as possible to the customer after the end of the month. A stringent and disciplined approach of follow up using letters, telephone conversations and personal visits should be used at your discretion to collect debts. It is not possible to describe a standard collection procedure as so much depends on the circumstances. In any case your cash collection procedure is personal to your business and so systems should be tailored accordingly. However it is clear that personal relationships play an important part in obtaining timely payment from your customer; generally telephone conversations and personal visits are more effective than impersonal reminder letters because informality, salesmanship and humour can be injected into such communication.

A great deal of time, effort and money can be saved in the inexorable task of debt collection if certain preventative steps are taken. Make sure that invoices are accurate and presented in the format required by the customer. This is especially true when dealing with government departments or large companies and in particular circumstances such as exporting, where considerable payment delays can be expected if documentary procedures are not strictly followed. Also take the trouble to find out your customer's payment procedure and timetable and send your invoice to the right location and preferably to a person known to you. In fact you and your staff should establish good personal working relationships with several of your customer's staff including the company accountant, payments clerk and buyer, in addition to the director or manager with whom you normally make contact.

52 How do I check a customer's credit-worthiness?

There are several sources of information that you can use to check the credit worthiness and financial position of your customers.

(a) **Your own sales ledger if the company is an existing customer.** This will reveal the facts about both the historical level of business with a customer which may indicate whether he is in growth or decline and also his payment record. If the payment record is consistent and within due dates then it is likely that your customer is not under financial strain, whereas erratic payments or round sum payments on account should be a warning signal to you.

(b) **Sales representative's report.** Your sales representative will usually be the first point of contact with a potential new customer. A standard report should be compiled by your representative giving the basic company facts such as name (including parent company name), address, type and size of business, bankers and trade references, details of the proprietor, etc.

This information provides you with an initial assessment and will help with your subsequent examination.

(c) **Directories and credit registers.** If you are continually dealing with many new potential customers it is worthwhile obtaining a directory of trading organisations giving basic company details and/or subscribing to a credit register. This will provide you with a preliminary inspection of credit-worthiness which may be sufficient for relatively small volumes of business.

(d) **Published accounts.** The published accounts and reports of companies available from Companies House or via credit bureaux provide a wealth of historical information on the trading performance, financial state and ownership of a company. The major drawback is that the information can be out of date. This is not the place to describe how to use a set of company accounts. If you require advice on how to interpret such information you should contact your accountant or financial adviser.

(e) **Credit bureaux reports.** In addition to published accounts you can obtain other credit information about your potential customer from credit bureaux, including a credit rating. This may comprise of a verbal assessment, classifications by payment record, opinions from suppliers with trading experience of the company and advice on trading at different credit values which often is quoted as a suggested credit limit. Written reports can take a week or two to compile but you can arrange for a verbal report by telephone in urgent cases. Clearly, in the latter case, the information may have to be confirmed so it is better to wait for fuller and probably more accurate information. The cost of a report can vary from between £5 and £40.

(f) **Trade references.** You should obtain a couple of trade references (given by current suppliers) from your prospective customer. Prepare a brief questionnaire which enables the referee to provide you with the facts of his recent trading experience with the customer and his opinion of credit-worthiness.

(g) **Banker's reference.** You can obtain from your prospective customer's bank a reference and assessment of credit-worthiness. The communication is often via your own bank and you can expect a charge for this service.

Ask specific questions, making reference to the level of credit you expect to advance. It is sensible to obtain advice from your own bank manager on the wording of any request you make.

Use bankers' references with caution: for example, 'a respectably constituted private limited company' means nothing more than that its bank account was opened in accordance with the reporting banker's normal procedures. Words such as 'fully committed' should be taken as a warning sign.

53 How should I set credit limits?

In checking the credit-worthiness of your prospective customers you have now received a wealth of information from both inside your company and from external agencies. Each of the sources of information will have recommended advice and even quoted figures in good faith to you concerning their opinion as to the credit-worthiness of your prospective customer. But the decision is yours to grant credit to your customer and to set the initial credit limit for new customers and to monitor the limits for existing customers.

Your credit risk with a customer is dependent on two credit limits:

(a) the amount of business carried out with a customer;
(b) the time limit for payment.

Clearly the overall credit risk is dependent on not only the volume of sales carried out with the customer but also the length of time that each of the debts remains unpaid.

Whilst it is appreciated that giving £3,000 credit involves a greater risk than giving just £1,000 credit to the same customer, it is not usually recognised that giving the £3,000 credit per month on 30 day terms is probably a lesser risk than giving the £1,000 credit per month on 90 day terms.

It is usually best to start a new customer on credit terms involving both a small amount limit and particularly a short time limit. This will ensure that you find out at the earliest date of any potential problems in collection. The credit limit can be reviewed regularly during the early months of trading to ensure that the limit remains at a reasonable level. When setting credit limits for your new customer try not to exceed the limits for trading suggested by the trade reference or credit bureau. It is important that customer credit limits are recorded clearly on the customer file and ledger card or contained on a computer file.

You should appreciate that the credit policy including credit limits and the terms of trading are an integral part of your business policy and in particular are strongly linked with the sales policy. It is important therefore that credit limits and credit policy are set with the knowledge and advice of the sales director. It is important that the sales staff are well informed of the overall business context in which their selling activity is based. Clearly some responsibility for potential bad debts rests with the sales team and they should be instructed in the importance of selling with a good credit risk.

Thus the credit limit that you set for each customer will finally depend on your judgement and commercial experience in balancing the desire for profitable business against financial risk. In a small growing company it is likely that this decision-making process will occupy a significant proportion of your time.

● **54 What do I do if a customer exceeds his credit limit?**

The key to this problem is to anticipate your customer's action and to be in possession of the latest facts regarding trading and payment. You should always try to take preventative action to avoid your customer exceeding the credit limit that you have set. This means that you should continuously monitor your customer's orders to make sure that when these are added to the existing debt this does not take them over the credit limit. Of course this will be more difficult in some trades (e.g. retailing) where your customer does not give notice of his intention to purchase but collects his goods and requests that his account is charged accordingly. Clearly in this situation it is most important for credit management to communicate to the selling staff a regular and up-to-date list of customers with whom care should be exercised. Consequently it is important to keep your customer accounts and debtors ledger regularly maintained and current to ensure they display the latest information. It is both embarrassing and a threat to your future trading relations with the customer to request payment for a debt which was settled the previous day.

Usually the most effective bargaining counter you have when a customer is requesting goods or services beyond his credit limit is to threaten to withhold supplies until suitable payment is made for previous debts. Clearly this action may prove very unpopular with your customer and your own sales staff and any such planned action should be carefully discussed with your sales staff before a decision is taken. This action normally results in immediate payment being made by the customer because he needs the goods or services. In this respect it is helpful to speak to the customer's buyer in the first instance and he will normally be able to arrange early payment. If you are supplying regular goods on a replacement basis then a suitable system for the collection of debts would be for your delivery driver to collect payment for the previous consignment as he delivers the latest or replacement consignment. If payment is not forthcoming then he should drive the goods away. But usually this threat will result in the payment being received in full.

The best way to achieve maximum sales volume without exceeding the credit limit is by fast collection of money and we have discussed the various ways of approaching this subject in answer to question 50. However as you develop the business, or as your customer requirements grow, then you will need to review and occasionally revise individual customer credit limits in the light of new information that is available about your customer's financial standing or in the light of your own trading situation and record of payment. Credit limits should never be allowed to remain dormant otherwise they will act as a continual brake on your business.

55 Can interest be charged on an overdue account? ●

Sometimes customers are slow in paying debts and accounts exceed the published and agreed terms of sale and consequently become overdue. One remedy here is to charge interest on overdue amounts but if this is the case then you should be sure that this is included in your standard terms of sale.

In the same way that your standard terms of payment are published on your sales order acknowledgement and your invoice and statement of account, it must be clearly stated that interest will be charged on overdue debts from a certain date and at a given interest rate.

It is not an established procedure to charge interest on overdue accounts but it is widespread in one or two trades. In general, it is not popular and is likely to lead to the loss of customers, therefore it should be dealt with in a careful manner.

It is in your own interest to check that such a procedure is adequately quoted and indeed highlighted on both your invoice and your statement of account. Moreover, if you wish to practice this procedure, then you must take a firm line to sue if your debtor refuses to pay interest. In general, it is better that preventative action is taken to stop debts becoming overdue. It is much easier and more effective to collect money in an amicable manner.

● 56 How can I prevent a debt going bad?

The longer the debt is outstanding the more likely it is to become bad. Incidentally, do not assume that all bad debts are a result of companies going into liquidation or individuals becoming bankrupt. Many of the bad debts that are written off in the company accounts are because of the stubborn refusal of debtors to pay amounts owing due to misunderstanding or dispute. In such circumstances the supplier will have assessed the situation and realised that the cost of recovery is going to render uneconomic any further pursuit of the debt.

In order to prevent a debt becoming doubtful or bad, it is important to take early steps with a good progressive credit control system. Firstly, know your customers and try to anticipate where problems may arise. Secondly, develop a good credit management reporting system which keeps you up-to-date. This will enable you to monitor the debts as they become overdue and take early action for recovery. Thirdly, if your normal credit control procedure of writing letters and making telephone calls does not bring about the required action from the customer, then you should threaten the withholding of supplies. Finally, if your customer does not require further supplies then probably the most effective remedy is to initially threaten and subsequently take legal action. Depending on the size of the debt, it is probably best to employ a solicitor or debt collection agency as they are experienced in the necessary procedures.

You can mitigate the loss through bad debts by insuring all or some of your debts with a credit insurance company. It is also possible to arrange excess insurance so that only balances in excess of a mutually agreed figure are insured by the company. In addition to normal domestic trade credit, this method of credit insurance is also available for export debts under the auspices of the Government's Export Credits Guarantee Department.

You can also try to reduce the risk of loss by inserting a clause in your standard conditions of sale retaining title to the goods until they have been paid for. However legal advice must be obtained as the validity of this option may be successfully challenged when you seek to rely on it.

57 Do I have to be a debt collector? •

It is understandable that after reading the answers to the previous seven questions you believe that your time is better spent running your business than chasing debts. Credit control and debt collection is a specialist function and you may prefer your business to be free of this aspect of detailed administration. There are several ways in which you can control credit effectively without doing it yourself.

(a) **Customer lease sales.** If you are selling equipment, machinery or another appropriate product, this method can be a very effective one in carrying out business. The financial institutions and leasing companies can provide facilities for your customer to purchase goods from you on a lease. The leasing company will assess the credit risk and accept the customer accordingly, after which you would normally receive full cash payment from the leasing company within a few days of sale. The leasing company administer the customer lease by instalments in the normal way. This method provides you with an attractive selling package of product plus available finance which should open up new sales opportunities.

(b) **Debt factoring.** This has become a popular method for suppliers to avoid the administration and risk of credit management and debt collection. There are two types; firstly, non-recourse factoring where the bad debt risk is covered by the factor and secondly, recourse factoring where the supplier bears the risk of bad debts. Both of these factoring types allow for the factor to purchase the debts at an agreed time in advance thus providing the majority (70% to 85%) of the finance at that time. This would normally cover the supplier's costs with the balance payable by the factor less a service charge when the debt is settled by the customer. The factor carries out the work involved in sales ledger accounting and credit control and makes a service charge. Make sure you are clear about how much the factor's services will cost: they can be expensive and, although in theory you should be relieved of administrative worries, accounting for transactions with the factor may become complicated.

(c) **Invoice discounting.** Using this method the supplier assigns the total debts immediately to the factoring company thus providing immediate finance in the form of an advanced payment. It is used essentially as a source of extra finance using trade debts as security rather than a credit control service. The supplier agrees with the factor a list of debts for sale and the factor pays an agreed proportion (around 70% to 80%) in advance. The balance is paid when the customer pays in full less the discounting charge. The credit management function is retained by the supplier whose customer is unaware that the debt has been discounted by a factoring company. Again, as with debt factoring, be aware of the cost and time needed to use this service efficiently.

(d) **Debt collection.** Whilst you may feel comfortable about retaining the main function of credit management within your business, it can be helpful to hand over the final debt collection task to a specialist. Occasionally you will have a debt which has defied your strenuous efforts to collect and you appear to have no alternative but to use the law. In these cases it is a good idea to use the services of either your solicitor (some of whom specialise in this type of work) or a specialist debt collection agency who carry out this task on a continuous basis for many companies. Alternatively, you can use the Small Claims Court.

10 PLANNING AND CONTROLLING PRODUCTION

● **58   What does production planning involve?**

Production planning is concerned with the allocation of resources to the manufacturing of goods. This field of activity incorporates information on production quantities, labour and machine availability and costs, and customer priorities.

With reasonable sales forecasting, many organisations can manufacture a quantity of goods for stock, so they are able to satisfy customer demand in the time it takes to process an order and distribute the product. But when goods are manufactured solely to order, decisions must be made on the priority of each order, the manufacture or purchase of components, the acquisition of raw materials, the use of overtime and so on.

The sequence and timing of manufacturing operations must be decided in order to create a production schedule, based on knowledge of machine speeds and operational timings. Where many machines are involved and many operations required, this function is often best performed by a computer.

Decisions must also be taken on whether to make or purchase components, in the light of cost and supplier lead times, special tooling requirements and additional plant loading for high priority items.

It is likely that material selection will be made when an order is received or on the provision of an estimate, but where this is not the case, appropriate materials must be selected before production can begin. Similarly, decisions on the number and grade of employees to be used on a particular job must be made.   -

Where production planning is computerised a master production schedule will be updated for each order. Where a manual schedule or T-card system (see next question) is maintained, it will be necessary to update the production plan to commit resources firmly. In the short-term most resources are finite; shift lengths may vary and additional shifts may be commissioned but the number of machines is usually only extendable by capital expenditure. Thus it is vitally important to commit adequate resources to each order.

The provision of work documentation will often be considered as part of the planning function. Although such documentation (e.g. route cards and works instructions) may often be created on receipt of an order, it will need to carry some time/sequential information in order that the production plan may be put into action.

In addition, actual time taken must be recorded, during or after the production process, so that future production planning may be undertaken with reasonable confidence in the accuracy of the operational timings used. Production control and recording actual production data are the keys to effective production planning.

59 How can I plan production?

Businesses often start with a light order book and slot each new order easily into available capacity. The only formal planning is to decide which goods to make first. As a company's order book becomes fuller, the influencing factors on what to make and when to make it become more complex; machines become loaded to capacity, component suppliers do not meet delivery schedules, key staff go sick and so on.

Many successful companies maintain their production plan on a T-card system. This offers an ordered methodology and will act as an *aide memoire* to constructive thought in the juggling act that production planning inevitably becomes.

The typical T-card system has a board with slots into which T-shaped cards can be inserted. Time (in months, days or shifts) can be recorded in one dimension of the board, whilst processes or plant can be recorded on another. The T-card (which represents a particular job or transaction) can be inserted into the appropriate machine slot on the correct day. As work builds up so will the Production Plan.

Where there are multi-level production processes a number of boards can be used in conjunction. Alternatively network, or critical path diagrams, can be created showing the logical relationships between processes to be used in conjunction with T-card systems. It is possible, even in the most complex manufacturing process, to record the sub-assembly steps towards the completion of a product in the order in which they are required.

Where informal methods of production planning are successful, i.e. where customers' orders are always fulfilled without undue high stock holdings, a move towards more formal methods is only necessary to ensure continuity and to provide a methodology for additional staff or at holidays.

As a company's order book expands, not only will the factors affecting the production schedule expand, but the impact of that schedule on other areas of the business will also be felt. Stock control, material requirements planning and even purchasing procedures will be affected until one person will not be able to cope with all of the implications of production planning. It is at this stage in a company's growth that a formal production plan will be necessary.

It is possible to use spreadsheets on microcomputers to maintain a production schedule, showing machines (or orders or customers) in columns and time periods in rows. Thus, a matrix of work to be performed against time allotted to it can be built up. Where a high priority job arrives in the schedule, all other jobs are automatically allocated a new time slot.

Even more sophisticated computerised scheduling facilities are available but these tend to be part of integrated production control systems, intended for use on microcomputers.

● **60 How do I decide what to make and when?**

At any time, a manufacturer is either producing to order or for stock. Where customer priorities demand that production is all to order then either nothing can be made for stock or additional resources are required.

Typically where sales forecasts provide for the holding of reasonable (i.e. cost justified) stock levels, it is to be hoped that stock issued to meet orders will be replaced by manufacturing of quantities pre-ordained for stock.

If business is brisk and you need to decide whether to manufacture to order or to make the required stock quantities, it is likely that commonsense will dictate you manufacture to meet the order book.

If business becomes even brisker, provision of additional resources for the long-term must be considered.

Such considerations are complicated where the end product is a composite structure requiring the manufacture of components as part of the ultimate assembly. Planning needs to take place before the start of the production lead time, when you are making to order. After looking at stock levels and planned production for stock, you can analyse the order into its component parts to give the net manufacturing requirements.

Determining the manufacturing requirement involves:
− sales forecasting;
− capacity planning;
− production planning;

in the creation of:
− master production schedules which show what is to be completed and when;
− bills of materials which show what constitutes each product;
− lead time schedules for products and components;
− stock schedules;
− machine loading schedules;
− labour requirements.

The satisfaction of customer orders (from stock or by manufacturing to order) is thus a composite exercise, utilising data from several sources. For example, if a product has a number of components, the longest lead time of which is several weeks, then production of that component, must clearly commence before the others. Schedules of stock for that component will also require attention well in advance of any others and cumulative lead times of components must also be taken into account, where the composite parts of components have long lead times. In deciding what to make, and when, the study of lead times is as important as the quantities involved.

61 How should I plan my materials requirements? ●

A master production schedule will provide a statement of the quantities of each end product due to be completed in a particular time period to help meet sales forecasts or stock requirements. You must bear in mind production capability and capacity when creating the master schedule. By analysing the production schedule into its component parts it is possible to work out a schedule of the material requirements for each run.

Other factors need to be taken into consideration, delivery lead times, overseas trade considerations and whether the supplier is a stockist or manufacturer, all will affect the quantity ordered. A material requirements schedule will enable you to prepare purchase orders either manually or by computer.

Some companies assess economic order quantities for particular stock items. Where these have been pre-set such orders will be recorded into the materials requirement schedule to achieve a happy balance of sufficient raw materials without overstocking.

Thus, by using the bills of materials, it is possible to dissect the master production schedule to obtain a gross material requirement. This schedule can then be converted into gross requirements per period, where lead times are known. If free stock and goods on order (see question 63) are also known you can calculate the net material requirement for the period.

● **62   What stock levels should I hold?**

Ideally, the stock levels of finished goods held should reflect customer demand. Stocks of Easter eggs in June have little immediate saleable potential. Where there is no seasonal fluctuation in demand for a product, past sales for a particular period are a useful guide to likely future sales. The intention should be to have sufficient stocks to satisfy customer demand without incurring the associated costs of overstocking.

Similarly, with raw materials, the aim should be to have sufficient stocks to meet production requirements without overstocking.

Where the production lead times are short, there is less danger in understocking finished goods and so incurring customer frustration. Analysis of previous sales, coupled with market knowledge, is frequently the only way in which to set sales forecasts. Sales forecasting is the responsibility of the sales department, and not the stores or accounts.

With knowledge of normal usage and production lead times, it is possible to create a realistic equation for stock levels:

average weekly usage × production lead time in weeks

For example, if 200 units are sold in an average week and it takes two weeks from placing an order on the factory to receiving the goods in stock, stock levels of 400 should be held. This does not take into account unexpected orders. Therefore, it is desirable to make provision for a buffer or safety stock.

The cost of understocking is not always quantifiable as the cost to the business of a lost customer is impossible to calculate. The cost of goods in stock and not sold (production costs plus overheads plus interest not received) is calculable. The buffer stock will vary between stock items. Similarly, the cost of damaged customer relations will be noticeably greater with some customers than with others.

There are other factors to be taken into consideration when setting the level of safety stock and hence total stock level. The order quantity of raw materials could affect batch sizes. Production scheduling could generate spare capacity that would be profitably taken up by producing for stock, even if that results in overstocking. But, despite such considerations, the essence of determining stock levels is that the level should cater for average usage and production lead times with a provision for a safety stock. Constant monitoring of stock levels will show whether the safety stock figure is correct.

Many businesses also have a 'servicing factor', whereby they decide what percentage of orders they wish to satisfy from stock. The factor is monitored and will generate a reduction or increase in stock levels according to how closely the servicing factor is met.

63 How do I keep stock records?

For both finished goods and raw materials, the issue and receipt procedures are the key to keeping accurate records of balances on stock. There are several different balances to be held against each stock reference number. The stock reference number can be designed to incorporate useful information such as product groupings, colour, style or location.

PHYSICAL stock is the quantity of an item actually in stores. ALLOCATED stock is that portion of the physical stock which is destined for use (either to a customer in the case of finished goods or to production in the case of raw materials). FREE stock is that physical stock which has not been allocated. STOCK ON ORDER is that quantity of an item which is on order and not yet received into stock.

Whatever the recording medium, and it could be either a manually maintained card system or a computerised system, the only way in which the information can be relied upon is to establish rigorous disciplines for recording issues and receipts. For example, issues may be requisitioned and the control could be a supervisor's signature on the requisition document, denoting that the stock record has been updated. A stores issued note could be used or, in the case of finished goods, despatch notes could be allocated a transaction number which would match a transaction on the stock records. In every case, there must be formal responsibility for the recording of stock movements. Receipts should be recorded in a goods received book.

In the case of both issues and receipts, the transaction document (i.e. stores issue note or despatch note, or goods received note) must be retained to serve as part of an audit trail, whereby stock transactions can be verified.

At scheduled intervals it will be necessary to undertake a physical stock check to verify the existence of the goods on the record card. Stock 'overs' or 'unders' will require investigation and the transaction documents should be totalled to give a picture of issues and receipts since the last physical stock check.

A stock record card should contain a description of the item, stock reference, supplier detail and, where applicable, physical location, e.g. bin number. The transaction detail, i.e. an issue or receipt, will include transaction number, quantity in or out and balance. A stock record on a computerised system would hold the same detail. However, it is only by establishing discipline over procedures that the records can be kept correct.

● **64   How do I identify and dispose of obsolete stock?**

A continuous system of appraisal for each type of stock should be instituted so that obsolete items can be identified. Obsolete stock will include, for finished goods, those which are no longer part of the product range, are no longer made to required standards, or those which, due to market forces, are not selling. A review of recorded stock quantities or a physical inspection of stock should highlight such circumstances.

Obsolete items of stock in raw materials or consumable stores will include materials specific to an obsolete finished goods item, per-

ishable goods, or consumable stores for items no longer on the inventory.

A continuous system of appraisal for both types of stock should set a time frequency whereby all stock items are evaluated over a year. If only a low number of stock items are held, this evaluation can be achieved successfully at the year end stock-take. If interim stock-takes are held, then a proportion of the stock items can be evaluated at this time.

This appraisal will involve examining each stock record to ascertain the date of the last movement; where movement frequencies are low (or possibly zero), the item should be listed as potentially obsolete. Management should review this list and direct which stock items are to be removed from the inventory and, where appropriate, disposed of.

Marketing, production and accounts departments should, of course, be consulted in order to assess the worth and value of particular items before disposal. In particular, the accounts department should advise on correct procedures for disposal of goods.

Some goods may be actively marketed as special offers, some placed for tender and some sold for scrap; the accounts department will need a system whereby any such sale is notified to them so that they can adjust their records.

● 65 Is the layout of my premises important?

Any space within a company costs money through rent, rates, lighting, heating and security. The inefficient use of such space has as significant an effect on the profitability of the organisation as a slow workforce or the scrapping of usable materials.

The layout of a factory or storage area can also directly affect the efficiency of the production or warehousing function. Excessive movement of materials requires extra labour whose cost must eventually be considered when determining selling prices and margins.

There are a number of factors that must be taken into consideration when preparing a suitable factory and/or warehouse layout:
– Where do raw materials enter and finished goods leave the factory?
– What is the manufacturing process involved and in which order is equipment required?
– Will materials be moved by forklift trucks and if so at what production/storage stage?

– Does any equipment require provision of power, water, compressed air, drainage, etc?

– Which machines, if any, require special access for servicing?

– Do any processes need special environmental conditions, nonstandard planning or vibration isolation mountings?

It may be necessary to make some compromises, particularly when a company is producing a range of products which are 'batch processed'. But, although solutions should be related to the majority of the throughput, low usage facilities should not be 'designed out' of the layout simply because they are too difficult to incorporate. An appropriate layout should assist the company in its efficient operation and not limit the product range.

66 Does the type of business I am in make a difference?

It most certainly does. In any industry it is likely that there will be special considerations which will require particular emphasis. But it is possible to make some general comments which may be an aid to improving profitability.

In a complex manufacturing environment, where most goods are made to order, the planning and control of schedules will involve a fine understanding of technical considerations. Deciding the precise sequence of operations is likely to be problematic where there is continuous batch production. The production planner will also need to record actual production data carefully for use in improving the planning performance.

Where the processes of manufacture are less complex, but where there are decisions about whether to manufacture or supply from stock, the importance of accurate sales forecasting can be observed. The marketing department of such an organisation will bear the brunt of not only predicting demand but also any seasonal fluctuations and close downs which should be reflected in the stock holding quantities.

Where a product is subject to fluctuations in demand, the forecasting of sales will require a blend of intuition and analysis. Where consistency of sales is achieved, the forecasting of future sales can be more accurate. An additional benefit of such stability will be that the accounts department can cost stock holdings accurately. A reduced investment in stock will lead to increased profitability where there is no conflict with the order book.

With a stable order book it is easier to keep records correctly, as calculations on work in progress, average order value and order administration costs can all be performed more easily.

One of the most useful ways to monitor product ranges and to increase profitability is to hold an interdepartmental meeting with the specific purpose of looking at stock. Even using a manual system it should be possible to review a sales analysis in conjunction with stock records from the points of view of the sales department, production planning and accounts. Inter-departmental co-ordination is certainly essential, whatever the type of business and such a meeting can help to ensure:

– economical stock holdings;
– customer satisfaction;
– accurate stock records and analysis.

Whilst production planning and its effectiveness will differ from industry to industry, it is possible to guard against areas where losses can occur. Constant watchfulness, accurate stock recording and physical stock-checks can guide the planner to redundant product lines. Constant monitoring of the product range and stock levels in any industry will improve profitability.

11 USING A COMPUTER

67   How do I decide if I need a computer?

A computer is just a tool. But deciding whether to use a computer is not about choosing the best machine. The objective is to decide whether it is right for your business; what, if any, jobs it might do; and what the value of any benefits that might arise from its purchase would be. Choosing the equipment is the last, and in some respects, the easiest part of the job.

Know what you want the computer to do before approaching suppliers. List the jobs, giving a breakdown of each, e.g. the invoices need to show delivery date, order number, price, discount, etc. Give each feature a priority value. Evaluate the volume of work for each job, the number of accounts, transactions, etc. Also give details of the flow of work and the daily, weekly, monthly and seasonal peaks and troughs.

Consider the computer's worth to your business. List the reasons, job by job, which you feel justify the use of a computer. Calculate the value of the benefits including the cost of achieving them (e.g. interest saved on an overdraft from a 10% reduction of inventory £3,500; less cost of one part-time stores clerk £2,000; net benefit £1,500. Total the potential benefits and compare them to the purchase cost and the running costs of the computer.

Unless a computer is going to increase your income or reduce your expenditure, think twice before purchasing one. Do not be swayed because others are using a computer. The most satisfactory reasons are likely to be tangible. Characteristic fallacies about the benefits of computerisation include:
- staff reduction (rarely happens);
- increased sales (machines do not sell things);
- improved service;
- reduction in stock levels;

– improved management information (who will use it and for what purpose).

A computer will not solve problems or give benefits just by itself. The benefits will arise only if you invest extra time and staff in using the information which the computer provides. You need to plan how to do this and consider the cost of doing it against the cost of the computer. There is also an added factor to consider – employee relations. Have you thought about the effects on your staff? How are you going to avoid unnecessary traumas which may occur because of the discipline demanded by the computer? However, discipline does have advantages; it means that it is easier for other people to take over someone else's job when they are ill or on holiday.

● **68   What is a computer?**

A computer is just a machine in which you store information (your business records) which you can then manipulate – add to, alter, print out – very rapidly.

A computer works like a clerk. You tell it how to do a job. It keeps these instructions (PROGRAM) in its MEMORY. It recalls them every time you ask it to do that particular job. Like the clerk, it has to be given work to do (INPUT). To do the job it may have to look up records previously stored in FILES. The computer's files are kept on magnetic DISKS. Just like the clerk, the computer carries out the job referring to its files and its input, and using its memory and its 'brain' (PROCESSING UNIT). When the job has been done, the end-product (an updated file or an invoice for example) remains for somebody to use (OUTPUT). You need to know only a few other words of computer jargon: BYTE – means character (letter, number, symbol); MEGA – means a million (megabyte; a million characters); K – means thousand; MICRO and MINI – small business computers – the differences are not important. Micro is the smallest – they are marketing terms as far as the non-technician is concerned; HARDWARE – the computer machinery; SOFTWARE – the programs that tell it how to work; DISKETTE – a small disk for use with small computers (sometimes called a floppy disk).

69 How do I choose a supplier?

You get what you pay for. Give preference to suppliers who are based in your area, have their own support staff, have an established business, have good references from other customers, have products from well-known and established manufacturers. Remember that many computer suppliers specialise in particular industries and trades. Choose a supplier who knows your business and has products specially adapted to meet its needs.

Get quotations from at least three suppliers. Deal formally with each supplier. Give each a written statement of your requirements and demand written proposals showing how each job can be done by the proposed product and stating how much it will cost. Ensure that each proposal is prepared in the same way to facilitate later comparison.

Check that each proposals covers *what* you want doing and do not get sidetracked by optional extras; do stick to your priorities. Do not get blinded by technology – it is *what* the computer will do that is important to you, not *how* it will do it. Compare prices and service levels. Choose the one that does most of the jobs you want at the lowest price, provided the supplier meets the criteria set out above.

If you are using a computer for the first time, try to avoid doing complicated things with it. Make use of packages of ready-written programs to do the more straightforward jobs such as order processing, stock recording, billing, sales, purchases and nominal ledger accounting and gross net payroll production.

Unless you like taking risks avoid:
– leading-edge technology: if it is new and unique let somebody more experienced sort out the teething troubles;
– specially written programs: wait until you have experience and a better understanding of what computers can do;
– anything which requires you to learn new skills: learn the skill first then get a computer to assit you if it is necessary.

70 How do I choose software?

The software is the most important part of the package you are buying. You must choose the software first and then the machine on which to operate it.

The starting point is to list all the things you want to do, as already explained in the answer to question 67. Armed with this list you can talk to suppliers and dealers. You should start by taking the salesperson through your list. Explain which things are vital to you and which things you are prepared to alter. For example, you might be looking for a payroll program that will handle the repayment of loans to staff. This may be something that is so important you are not prepared to buy the program unless it has this facility.

When the dealer has suggested some programs that might be suitable, ask to see a demonstration. Ask the demonstrator to show you how the program handles all the things on your check list. Do not just glance at a standard demonstration designed to show off the best features of the program; try and use it yourself. Also find out whether the program will handle your volumes of records and transactions, will work fast enough to meet any deadlines you have and will still be suitable if the business grows.

Shop around and see several dealers and programs before making up your mind. Ask for written quotations and written answers to your questions about what the program does and how it meets your needs.

Remember that thousands of ready-written programs exist and usually there should be one somewhere that will meet your needs. It is always best to use ready-written programs because usually they are tried, tested and fully documented. If you have programs written specially, you they will be bound to find errors in them during the first months of use. They will also be very expensive. So, if a dealer suggests you have something specially written for you, do not say yes until you are certain that nobody has a program which fulfils your requirements.

For a fuller explanation of business software, read the *Daily Telegraph's* book, *How to Choose and Use Business Microcomputers and Software.*

● 71   What types of software are there?

A last word about choosing software. Software comes in several categories:
– applications packages: sets of programs to handle specific jobs like sales ledger, billing, payroll;
– report writers: a program that lets you select information from your files and print it out in the format you specify; a useful tool for

producing special reports you may only need once in a while (warning: you will need lots of time to teach yourself how to use this facility);
– spreadsheet packages: a program that lets you set up rows and columns of figures and headings and specify how each is calculated or totalled – for example, a list of products and prices and the expected sales you will make in the next twelve months:

Product	Price	Sales Target											
		1	2	3	4	5	6	7	8	9	10	11	12
1	1.50	100	100	100	100	100	100	100	100	100	100	100	100
2	2.00	200	100	200	100	200	100	200	100	200	100	200	100
3	1.00	1000	1000	1000	1000	1000	1000	1000	1000	1000	1000	1000	1000
4	3.00	50	100	50	100	50	100	50	100	50	100	50	100

You can put in a formula which gets the program to calculate the value of sales each month (monthly sales = quantity sold × price) and the total value of sales in the year for each product and the total sales of all products each month.

Product	Sales Value in Month												
	1	2	3	4	5	6	7	8	9	10	11	12	Total
1	150	150	150	150	150	150	150	150	150	150	150	50	1800
2	400	200	400	200	400	200	400	200	400	200	400	200	3600
3	1000	1000	1000	1000	1000	1000	1000	1000	1000	1000	1000	1000	12000
4	150	300	150	300	150	300	150	300	150	300	150	300	2700
Total	1700	1650	1700	1650	1700	1650	1700	1650	1700	1650	1700	1650	20100

Once this is set up, you can change the values and the computer program will automatically recalculate everything. You can sit and work through all your options, asking 'what if I . . . ?' with very little effort after first setting up your report.
– word-processing packages: program your computer for computerised typing allowing text to be stored in files and re-used at will and altered without the whole of a document having to be retyped.

When choosing software, the applications packages are the important things. The other types of programs are useful optional extras but rarely important enough to condition your choice of computers.

72   Is there a program to suit my business?

There are thousands of ready-written programs to do most of the things you are ever likely to think of.

In the next few pages we list some of the types of business we have helped in using computers in the last few years, followed by a list of uses to which you can put computers. Neither is comprehensive, but it indicates the range of things you can do in case you still think it is not worth shopping around to find the dealer who can help you.

Examples of the types of business for which specialised software is available:

Accountancy
Advertising and sales promotion
Aerospace and airline services
Agriculture
Architectural
Banking, finance and property
Bookmakers
Booksellers
Breweries and brewing
Broadcasting
Broking
Building industries
Builders merchants
Building societies
Car hire
Cartography
Catering
Charities
Chemical
Civil engineering
Cleaning contractors
Clothing
Commodity books and dealing
Communications
Construction
Container handling
Contractors
Credit card accounting
Defence
Dentistry
Department stores
Despatch services
Domestic appliances
Educational
Employment agencies

Energy – public sector
Engineering
Estate agents and chartered surveyors
Estate management
Farming
Film industries and television
Food and drink
Foundry
Garment trade
Glass processing
Government
Grain traders
Hospitals and health care
Hotels
Insurance and life houses
Jewellers
Leasing companies
Legal profession
Libraries
Local authorities
Motor trade
Music publishing
Newsagents wholesalers
Oil
Paint manufacture
Paper
Pension groups
Pharmaceutical
Plant hire
Ports
Property management
Publishing
Quantity surveyors
Record and music industry

Retailing
Sewage engineers
Shipbuilders
Shipping/freight
Ship management
Steel
Stockbroking
Structural engineering
Textiles
Timber
Toy manufacture

Trade unions
Transport
Travel and travel agencies
Typesetting
Universities
Veterinary surgeons
Warehousing and packaging
Waste disposal
Water authorities
Wines and spirits

Examples of Applications Software
Purchase ledger
Sales ledger and sales analysis
Addressing, mailing and alpha indexing
Assets accounting
Auditing
Billing (order entry, sales order processing, sales invoicing, etc.)
Bills of materials
Distribution (transport management, warehousing, freight forwarding, etc.)
Employee benefit administration
Export and import administration
Finance planning and modelling (including demand forecasting, etc.)
General ledger (nominal ledger and financial reporting)
Hire purchase, rental and lease accounting
Integrated accounting systems
Inventory control
Investment management and accounting (bonds, stocks, shares, etc.)
Job and product costing
Numerical control
Payroll
Pensions
Performance analysis and planned maintenance (labour, machines, materials etc.)
Personnel (including aptitude testing)
Production and process control
Project management

Purchasing
Stockholder accounting (share registration, dividends)
Tax administration
Telephone usage analysis
Text processing (including cataloguing and typesetting)
Time recording and accounting
Word processing

● **73 Where can I find out more?**

If you want to find out more about computer programs for your industry and type of business then you should ask at your local library for copies of the following reference books which contain lots of suppliers, services and products.

1 NCC, The National Centre for Information Technology *Computing Decisions* (The Kemps Group Jan. 1985).

2 *How to Choose and Use Business Microcomputers and Software* (Telegraph Publication Jan. 1985).

Alternatively, you can buy one of the many periodicals aimed at the business user of microcomputers, for example, *Which Micro, PC User* and *PC Management.* These are available in most newsagents.

12 PEOPLE

74 How do I decide how many people to employ? ●

Where the activities and scale of the organisation are already known, the decision on how many people to employ is governed mainly by the nature of the work and the work content involved in the various activities. Any error in staffing levels should be readily apparent from, for example, the build-up of work at a bottleneck. Once you are satisfied that an overload is likely to persist unless action is taken, the type and number of additional staff needed can be decided in the light of where the back-log occurs, the rate of build-up and the rate of work clearance.

Where the organisation is not yet in operation, to estimate the number of people required involves first identifying the activities required to meet the objectives of the organisation, breaking these down into tasks that can be allocated to people, and then estimating the time involved in carrying out each task and the volume of work. It will almost always be worthwhile estimating the highest and lowest likely values. You should then aim at a staffing level marginally below the mid-point, if you are reasonably certain that you could recruit additional staff in an acceptably short time.

In either case, you will need to watch a number of points that otherwise could prove difficult to correct at a later stage.

Firstly, the work rate that is the 'norm' in one organisation can differ significantly from the 'norm' in another organisation. Raising this level once it has become 'accepted' can call for an unusually high level of goodwill on the part of the staff. The situation is best avoided by trying to ensure that the work rate is even between employees and of a satisfactory level before engaging further people. Question 80 refers to staff performance.

Secondly, since most businesses experience some seasonality, a manufacturer should work out the relative costs of allowing stocks to build up in order to maintain a steadier level of activity and constant number of staff, or keeping stock levels lower and varying the number of staff to match demand. For similar reasons, a retailer might benefit from employing enough full-time staff to meet the general level of work throughout the working week and then employing part-time staff, if practicable, to cope with the weekly and seasonal peaks. If you are in a service industry, consider how long this increased business will continue and, if practicable, employ temporary staff.

Finally, before taking on additional staff, look carefully at the possible effects of new technology. You may not need to increase your staff numbers, but rather to invest in equipment and retraining.

● **75 How do I recruit staff?**

Recruiting is not simply a matter of seeing a few people and selecting one. Costly errors are best avoided by adopting a systematic approach to recruitment.

Initially, it is important to decide whether there is a real recruitment need. If you establish that recruiting new staff is the only way to overcome a problem, there are three essential steps you should take.

Step 1 – Prepare a job description identifying:
- how the job fits into your organisation and its main purpose;
- who the job holder reports to;
- who reports to the job holder;
- the job duties and responsibilities in clear terms.

Step 2 – Prepare a candidate specification indicating:
- the preferred age range;
- the required qualifications;
- the practical experience required;
- any personal qualities you are looking for, e.g. non-smokers or clean driving licences.

Step 3 – Establish the conditions of employment covering:
- salary, taking market and internal forces into account;
- fringe benefits, i.e. car, pensions and private health cover;

- assistance you will give with relocation;
- the period of notice to be given by both parties.

After you have prepared the background data, which will help in clarifying your thoughts as to the proposed recruitment and in preparing for your interview discussions, advertise the post:
- internally, to encourage a merit-based promotion system; and/or
- externally, using advertising media appropriate to the job description in question and geographical area to be covered.

Once you have a supply of potential candidates for interview, be courteous to them by keeping them informed regularly as to how their application is progressing.

During the interview process, use a structured approach to ensure that all candidates are interviewed in a similar manner and that all aspects are covered for all candidates. Be careful not to go against the provisions of the Equal Opportunities and Race Relations legislation. In particular:
- supply the candidate with written information regarding the job duties and conditions of employment as an aid to discussion;
- explain how the proposed job fits into the business and what promotion prospects are possible;
- remember to point out any less attractive aspects of the job;
- test the candidate's technical ability by posing real situation questions and finding out why they have handled previous situations in a certain manner;
- determine relevant domestic issues, i.e. are there relocation problems for spouse or children at school and, if necessary, apply a personality test;
- allow ample time for the candidate to pose questions and answer them.

When you have compared the interviewed candidates with your candidate specification, use your judgement with whatever considerations you wish to apply then select the preferred candidate. Identify a second possible candidate in case the favourite applicant decides not to accept your offer; this will save additional costs should a further recruitment exercise become necessary.

Make an offer in writing which sets out the conditions of employment, include a job description as an appendix, and offer the post subject to references and other aspects you require, such as medical or security clearance. Do not mention 'probation periods' – they can be expensive.

Once the appointment is offered, agreed and satisfactory references obtained (often best by telephone), make sure a start date for the new employee is known and communicated to other staff. This will assist during the new employee's induction period. Subsequently, at say three, six or twelve months' service, review the employee's performance against the job description to:
– ensure you have the right employee for the job;
– assist you in any subsequent recruitment exercise.

Issue and post a notice just ahead of the new recruit's arrival telling everyone of the appointment and wishing the newcomer well. It will cost so little and do so much good to help them to settle in and begin making an effective contribution. If your initial recruitment exercise does not provide the candidate you want – repeat it. If you recruit in haste you will almost certainly repent at leisure.

● 76 How do I decide what qualifications and experience are necessary?

In general, what matters most is the ability of a candidate to do the job in question. Some jobs, of course, call for particular, specified qualifications to comply with statutory requirements, as for example in the case of Company Secretary, a medical officer/nurse or the driver of a heavy goods vehicle. Otherwise, it is the knowledge and skills the candidate has acquired – whether by academic achievement or practical experience (or both) – that matters rather than that they should meet some pre-determined and possibly arbitrary background requirement.

Qualifications provide a useful indication of the range of subject interest of the applicant as well as the depth of understanding of the principles of the subjects studied. Some would also suggest that they provide an indication of the personal qualities of the individual, in particular of proven perseverance, tenacity and the implied discipline.

Experience, on the other hand, indicates the range of actual working environments encountered. Success proves that skills have been acquired and applied. Admitted failures can also be useful experience, if only to recognise that pitfalls exist.

In drawing up a specification for a job holder, a good starting point is to decide and distinguish between what knowledge and skill levels are essential and desirable from the moment of joining and what will be necessary later.

When the job already exists and a replacement is being sought, a useful method of getting the answers to these questions is to establish, by asking rather than assuming, what other satisfactory job holders have had, and what unsatisfactory job holders have lacked.

Finally, a word about qualifications and their implications. In general it is best to determine and specify what minimum academic levels of attainment are essential so that a response can be expected from a wide range of applicants. The nature of some jobs, for example an analytical chemist, will determine what subjects and levels are necessary. But how do you take into account the number of subjects and the standard attained? And how are degrees and diplomas to be rated? Sometimes the highest attainments are less appropriate because while such a lively mind may identify new solutions more swiftly, it can also result in the individual losing interest in the job if it involves a significant routine element, or in the tendency to put more effort into discovering alternatives than into completing an assigned task. Either situation could lead to the individual leaving after a short period, possibly with information, knowledge and skills useful to a competitor.

● 77 Do staff need to be organised formally?

To achieve his objectives, a manager has to organise, by grouping activities logically and establishing effective working relationships between his subordinates.

Very occasionally a group of people work well together without formal organisation. This tends to happen, however, only where the group is small and the objective both clear and single. Under these conditions each person tends to make best use of their attributes. Once they know the objective, they can work together with the minimum of communication.

More frequently, when more than two or three people are engaged in working towards an objective that can be broken down into a number of tasks, formal organisation becomes necessary. Individuals may place a different level of importance on each of the areas of work and while some tasks might be duplicated, others could be overlooked. In all but the simplest of cases, therefore, work should be organised in a structured way.

Good organisation means objectives will be met because:
– all the individual activities necessary to meet the objectives are completed;

– each task is carried out effectively and efficiently by someone suited to the work;

– the rate of work enables the agreed time objectives to be met;
It is typified by a situation in which:

– everyone concerned knows the overall objectives;

– each individual knows what they are expected to achieve, and what their limits of authority and responsibilities are;

– no conflicts arise because more than one person has been asked to do the same task;

– no task 'falls between stools'.

Organising formally involves a number of key steps:

Step 1 – Define the objective. Record this in writing if necessary.

Step 2 – Define the work to be done. Again it might help to write this down.

Step 3 – Group related work. So that tasks can be carried out by the appropriately skilled staff with a minimum of movement.

Step 4 – Establish the span of control, that is, how many people should be reporting directly to the manager. In general this should be as many as practicable so as to reduce communication problems. The number will be smaller as the inter-relationship between the work of the subordinates becomes more complex.

Step 5 – Prepare a job description for each job so that everyone knows the extent of their responsibilities.

When reorganising becomes necessary, enlist help and encourage constructive comments from the people involved. They will know the details well, and help to ensure that there are no cases of things 'falling between stools'.

As the manager, explain your purpose and why you plan to organise in the way you have selected. If your ideas are sound and your explanation clear, you will get ready agreement and the satisfaction of knowing that things will carry on in your absence (in the short-term at least) satisfactorily and on the right lines.

If your ideas are not readily accepted, what are the preferred ideas? Are they acceptable? In fact – are they better? If they are, then accept them gracefully, acknowledge the fact openly, and you will be rewarded by work done well, with commitment and some pleasure.

● 78 How should I delegate work?

Delegating is a key task of a manager and subordinates often 'rate' their manager by reference to how well, or poorly, he does so.

In delegating, the manager should aim to be clear and precise so that there is no room for misunderstanding in relation to the objectives, and the scope for discretion. The manager should also make sure that adequate time is allowed for the task to be completed properly. People tend to react unfavourably when they are called upon to undertake at short notice a task that they believe could have been delegated to them much earlier, had it not been left on the manager's desk un-actioned.

People often interpret words and emphases differently so, wherever the slightest possibility of a misinterpretation exists, it is always best to have the subordinate 'repeat back' the requirement in his own words. Eventually, once a 'working relationship' has been developed, this becomes less necessary. In particular, the priority of the new task in relation to the subordinate's existing work should be discussed and agreed.

Where the subordinate is a manager, it will be necessary for you to assure him that he has adequate authority to take actions necessary to carry out the delegated task successfully, or knows clearly the limits of his authority.

If you hesitate to delegate, ask yourself 'Why?' Is it because:

(a) You have not the wish, the skill or courage?

(b) You have not the necessary confidence in your subordinate(s)?

If you believe you have not the skill, or lack the courage to delegate, identify a small task and a suitable subordinate, think out carefully how you are going to explain what you require – write it down if this helps – and then grasp the nettle. Call your subordinate, explain what is needed and why, making sure that you have covered all the points referred to above. The skill will come with practice.

If the problem is one of a lack of confidence in your subordinates, and there is a recurring need, you should consider what training they need and take steps to provide it.

Where the subordinate is a manager, his development is a main motivation in itself. For their own job satisfaction and sense of job security, many managers need to know that they are still receiving training. When you have competent, trained staff you can delegate with confidence.

79 Should I insist that work is formally planned and recorded? •

Planning involves determining the steps by which an objective can be achieved. Time is usually an important factor and a plan therefore needs stages and times for the completion of each stage. It follows that a manager cannot plan without knowing:
- the activities and tasks involved;
- the work content of each task;
- the resources available;
- the constraints.

A manager cannot achieve results unless a route has been found through to the objective and the activities have been thought through systematically. Network planning has become recognised as an essential tool to the successful planning of all but the most simple tasks and has been proven to be a highly effective means of ensuring that work is properly co-ordinated. It also provides a practical basis for ensuring that resource limitations, affecting the availability of particular skills and equipment, for example, are taken into consideration during the planning stage. In this way, planning can be a positive aid to the development of confidence of staff, so that a task can be completed by a required date, and is likely to be completed without being affected by avoidable delays.

Completion of each stage of the work should also be recorded promptly in order to give an up-to-date picture of the work. When doing this, it is advisable to record progress in the same planning units as those used in the compilation of the plan. Thus, if a task estimated to take seven hours has been completed, this number of hours should be deleted from the overall time estimate rather than the five or nine hours the task may in fact have taken. For the same reason, as work nears its completion, it is often helpful to measure progress in terms of percentages, in the secure knowledge that everyone recognises when a task is 100% complete. For payment purposes, on the other hand, and for the benefit of improving future estimates, it remains necessary also to record the actual time taken.

● 80 Should I try to measure the performance of my staff?

'If you can't measure it, you can't improve it!' Those were, more or less, the words of Lord Kelvin, the eminent nineteenth-century scientist. Certainly it is useful to have some measure of performance so that you can see and demonstrate whether a change has been for the better.

Some kinds of work can be measured much more easily than others. For example, work resulting in the production of goods is generally simple to measure and the results accepted as objective because the measurement can be expressed easily in terms of units per hour. The measurement of quality of production, though less easy to carry out, is also possible and usually necessary.

Other kinds of work are much more difficult to measure, for example, the work of a design draughtsperson, a quality control inspector, or where the work is of a clerical, technical and supervisory nature. The problem is also greater where the output is not easily related to the job holder's input, for example, as with a research worker where the results of a test may not be known for a number of years.

Manual work measurement techniques have been established for some time. The simplest involves, essentially, the use of a stop-watch and recording the time taken to complete a production cycle. Most recurrent manual work can also be estimated with adequate accuracy for planning purposes by the use of synthetic standards developed over the years and now readily accepted by management and unions as sound. The trend has been very much away from the use of a stop-watch and towards the use of synthetic standards.

Clerical work measurement until the late 1970s had always been regarded as a much more difficult proposition, mainly because clerical work involves so many different activities, some or most of which – such as thinking – are difficult to observe and hence record. Systems have, however, been developed for manual work; for example, an overseas institution has a system that clerks can apply themselves. In its current form, only the number of times some five activities are carried out need be known in order to establish the time for completing a clerical procedure: this provides data which is accurate enough for planning and establishing the number of people needed to carry out a given volume of work.

Frequently, aspects of performance other than 'output volume' are at least as important. Chief among these are the quality of the work produced and the excellence of the service provided. In establishing measures in these areas it is important to take account of the factors that matter most to those who are the users of the products or services provided. Some useful measures have included, for example:

– speed of turn-round/response to customers' requests;
– number of errors detected per day;
– number of complaints from customers regarding incorrect deliveries.

When setting performance standards, always involve your staff. It provides a unique opportunity to review the factors affecting performance and what can be done to make further improvements, against a background of what the 'end users' take into account in judging your staff's performance.

81 How do I decide the right amount to pay people?

Pay is one of the most difficult business equations to balance. Pay too little and there is an adverse effect upon staff motivation. Pay too much and there is an adverse effect on profits.

Many organisations claim that their human resource is their greatest asset. Quite often it is also their greatest single cost element. In such cases, an 'error' of only 1% can amount to a very significant sum. Accordingly, decisions on pay merit careful managerial attention.

In general, setting the pay of an individual involves taking decisions on three main factors:

– the basic relative worth of the job when performed adequately;
– the performance of the particular individual; and
– the potential of the individual to undertake more demanding work.

Basic Relative Worth
The basic worth of a job in relation to others is best established by job evaluation. Many methods are available.

The simplest schemes involve classifying jobs in accordance with definitions covering the range of jobs in question. This approach can be highly cost-effective so long as the jobs are all of one kind. Clerical and administrative jobs, for example, can sometimes be covered very adequately by a ready-made scheme such as that developed by the Institute of Administrative Management. Problems with classification systems arise, however, where jobs do not wholly and neatly fit into any one class.

A second method makes use of the 'paired comparison' technique, in which each job is compared with all other jobs systematically. The method produces results that are generally felt to be fair. It is simple to use and adequate if a relatively small number of jobs are involved. However, it does not indicate the extent of the difference between jobs, nor enable new and changed jobs to be evaluated consistently.

Where more than 20 to 30 jobs are involved, or where the range includes jobs of different types, an analytical method is the most satisfactory. The more easily understood and readily accepted methods analyse jobs under a number of headings ('factors') covering the knowledge, experience, mental, social and physical demands each job places upon its holder, and the responsibility and circumstances associated with the job. This approach enables jobs of widely differing types and levels to be evaluated within the same scheme.

Setting Basic Pay Levels

Having established the relativities between jobs internally, most organisations group together in a series of grades, largely to simplify pay administration. The pay for a grade can be at a single rate or cover a band.

In arriving at appropriate pay levels it is obviously important to take account of competitive rates. The rates for jobs held by people who could work at other local organisations clearly should be comparable. These are best established by making direct contact and asking, taking care to ensure that comparisons are based on the facts about the job demands, rather than on the titles of the jobs. (In the case of secretarial and supervisory jobs, the same job title may cover three or even four grades.)

For the more senior positions, where a job holder is more likely to make comparisons with a company elsewhere in the country, it is again best to make contact with the companies from which existing staff have been recruited or which employees have joined recently.

In both cases it is important to establish and to take account of:
- the ranges of pay, wherever these exist;
- the scale review dates.

It is also important to establish how you wish to compare with other comparable organisations, that is, at or above the general level. If you pay above, you will get a better response when recruiting, possibly hold on to your staff longer, but run the risk of leaving them 'locked in', that is feeling they want to leave, but are unprepared to take the drop in pay. It may also result in inadequate staff turnover for there to be a continuing in-flow of 'fresh blood' and new ideas.

Performance
Where the job holder can influence his output, there may be merit in recognising the fact by relating some portion of the total pay to the performance of the individual.

In the case of a banded pay structure, the 'width' of the band in relation to the basic pay should reflect how much more an excellent performer is worth than someone doing the same job to a 'just satisfactory' standard.

Many methods of relating pay to performance have been developed, each meeting particular requirements. When selecting a scheme, take care to examine and consider the acceptability of the variation in pay level to the employee and its size in relation to the basic or 'fall-back' level. What would happen in times of low activity? Will the scheme result in reduced unit costs? What will it cost to administer?

82 What if the market rate for the job is higher?

While it is always possible to develop a pay structure that will match the needs in most parts of an organisation, occasionally the level of pay appropriate to the grade of a particular type of job may not be sufficient to attract, retain and motivate staff of adequate calibre. In these circumstances, the pay level may need to be supplemented by lifting the level of pay appropriate to the grade by a 'market premium' sufficient to bring the total level to the prevailing 'going rate'. When this action is necessary, it is important for the job to retain the grading established by job evaluation, identify the job as exceptional and ensure that action is taken to review the size of the premium regularly.

● 83 How should I motivate my staff?

The implication of this question is that the staff are not motivated currently. If this really is the case, you will want to take effective steps to improve matters rapidly.

Pay and Motivation

To many people, including many managers, motivation is simply and directly a matter of pay. Yet most practising managers will confirm that any increase in pay often has a very short-lived beneficial effect on people's motivation. Only where an employee's pay is in some degree directly related to his work output, will performance be improved for any length of time. And even then, if the portion of pay that is related to output does not vary much, with the passage of time it usually gets consolidated with the basic pay so that any motivational effect it may have had is lost.

Pay, nevertheless, can have a very marked effect on motivation. If anyone feels that their pay is unfairly low – usually in relation to another fellow employee – his motivation will most certainly be affected adversely, and often to a degree out of all proportion to the extent of the difference he believes to exist. This finding seems to apply at all levels, within all organisations. In essence, pay can be a powerful de-motivator when it is believed to be unfair, but the converse is by no means true: pay above the 'felt-fair' level will always be gratefully accepted, but generally without any sustained improvement in performance.

Factors Affecting Motivation

In practice there tend to be two sets of factors that affect motivation: one that can hold people back from giving of their best, and a second that leaves staff feeling that they want to extend themselves, to do their best and show what they can do.

The de-motivating factors tend to include all those aspects of jobs that people regard as unsatisfactory and, unless they feel unable to speak their mind, could be expected to complain about. The most prevalent, recurrent complaints include:

– lack of clarity about objectives – not knowing what is expected of them;

– not knowing about matters about which they believe they should have been told;

– administrative procedures that seem cumbersome, inexplicably detailed and lengthy;

- work that is 'chopped and changed' for no apparent good reason;
- a work load that varies greatly where they suspect that, with better planning, the rushes and pauses could be avoided;
- an uncaring manager or management team;
- not being noticed;
- not being treated fairly – especially in terms of pay.

The motivating factors, conversely, are those which tend to leave staff feeling pleased. Chief among these tend to be:
- pride in their organisation;
- interesting work;
- the satisfaction of having their views sought;
- having the opportunity to do things their own way – making some decisions for themselves;
- having the satisfaction of knowing that the company is interested in their future by investing in training them;
- having a manager who takes a personal interest and helps where possible;
- having a manager who explains things so that they understand the reasons for decisions and instructions.

The number of factors can be many, often 50 or more. In one particular study that the writer carried out for an organisation where middle/senior management lacked motivation, he identified separate factors relating to the job, the company and the 'pay and conditions'. In each case the effect of the factor on the individual members of staff was recorded. The result was an 'action plan' that listed the top ten factors in a 'batting order'. The problems were not new or unknown, but had persisted because a main problem was knowing where to start. Having a batting order helped focus attention and, in a short period, resulted in real improvements. The two main problems were:
- lack of clear understanding of their own boss's objectives;
- belief that pay relativities were unfair.

Taking Action
Do not assume that eliminating a negative factor will always result in higher motivation. Unpleasant working conditions and poor light, for example, could lower performance, but improving these would not necessarily result in increased motivation. On the other hand, increasing the positive factors – or introducing these where previously they have been lacking – usually results in a real and lasting improvement.

107

Improvement in the motivation of staff begins by asking questions and securing involvement. A common mistake is to assume that you know the answers and take actions accordingly. Taking the first step of asking why motivation seems below par , will of itself, have a motivating affect that will last if you achieve something as a result.

Fun, Glory and Non-financial Incentives
Little to date has been written about the place of fun at work. Yet as people tend to do what they enjoy best, why not foster a sense of enjoyment at work.

Most people take pleasure in receiving praise for their achievements and work done especially where this has been hard-earned and where the praise is given by someone for whom they have respect. Sometimes it can cause even greater satisfaction when the word of praise is spoken in the hearing of others and where the written commendation is brought to the attention of others.

Praise costs nothing – save a little time and thought!

Additional Demands on the Manager

Improving the motivation of staff thus involves talking with them, working with them and securing their commitment to the work. It involves a style of management that will make additional demands on you.

Example plays a vital part; therefore, you must also set and maintain the example of self-motivation, enthusing your staff with your own genuine enthusiasm.

13 TRAINING

84 Why is training necessary?

Whatever the size of your business, people will be an important part of it. But people can create difficulties which prevent you from running your business profitably. Some examples of problems with personnel include:
– faulty goods, damaged machinery, lost production, accidents and lost sales opportunities caused by inefficient or under-trained staff;
– staff shortages – not enough people with the right skills available in the marketplace. And those you employ seem dissatisfied; they often stay away from work or there is a high turnover of employees.

These problems are frequently caused by people not knowing what their job is or what is expected of them. The answer to these problems could be in training, done either 'on-the-job' or through courses.

'On-the-job' training is learning by watching others do the job. It can be effective but it has several drawbacks:
– it can be a slow process;
– there may not be a suitable person to learn from. Or your selection may not be a good teacher, discouraging the trainees and giving them bad habits;
– where are the new ideas and improvements going to come from?

Training courses have none of these drawbacks. Skills and knowledge are taught systematically and quickly; the trainees are specialists in teaching and will pass on the best working methods and introduce new ideas and practices.

85 What training is needed?

To answer this question you will need to look at each person's job in your business, including your own.

Consider:
- what skills and knowledge are needed to do the job;
- what skills and knowledge will be needed in the future;
- what skills and knowledge does the current job-holder have.

The difference between current skills and knowledge and those needed shows what training is necessary. Although each business is different, a typical training programme might include:
- understanding finance and accounts;
- the skills of selling, including negotiation, presentation and letter writing;
- shop-floor skills involved in the production process including safety procedures;
- man-management – motivational skills, staff appraisal and interviewing.

● **86 How do I start to organise training?**

You may want to employ your own training officer to organise training for you. But, if you do not, there are many organisations who offer training by means of public or 'in-house' courses. A major source of training is the statutory Industrial Training Boards. The present bodies are:

Clothing and Allied Products – 10th Floor, Tower House, Merrion Way, Leeds LS2 8NY (0532-441331)

Construction – Radnor House, 1272 London Road, Norbury, London SW16 4EL (01-764 5060)

Engineering – 41 Clarendon Road, Watford, Herts WD1 1HS (0923-44322)

Hotel and Catering – PO Box 18, Ramsey House, Central Square, Wembley, Middx HA9 7AP (01-902 8865)

Offshore Petroleum – Forties Road, Montrose, Angus DD10 9ET (0674-72230)

Plastics Processing – Halesfield 7, Telford, Shropshire TS7 4QL (0952-584466)

Road Transport – Capitol House, Empire Way, Wembley, Middx HA9 0NG (01-902 8880)

There is also an Agricultural Training Board – Bourne House, 32/34 Beckenham Road, Beckenham, Kent (01-650 4890).

Further details can be obtained from the boards. Many of the boards issue training recommendations, publications and offer consultancy advice as well as running training courses. Grants are available from some boards towards the cost of programmes run by individual firms.

Some boards organise group training schemes where several businesses get together to share training resources. Many other boards were abolished in 1981. Their work has been taken over by voluntary training groups.

Other sources of training and training information are:

BACIE (British Association of Commercial and Industrial Education) – 16 Park Crescent, London W1N 4AP (01-636 5351). BACIE runs courses in a variety of subjects and can provide details of many courses run by other bodies.

The Industrial Society – 3 Carlton House Terrace, London SW1Y 5DG (01-839 4300). The Society runs courses (public and 'in-house') and offers advice and a range of publications.

The Manpower Services Commission – Moorfoot, Sheffield S1 4PQ (0742-703838). The Commission runs a variety of schemes and training programmes many of which are aimed at the small or the new business.

Finally, your professional advisers: solicitors, accountants and management consultants are often a useful source of external training both in 'off-the-shelf' and 'tailor-made' courses.

87 Can I get help with the cost of training?

Many of the training boards mentioned in the previous question pay maintenance and travelling allowances to people attending approved courses. They also make grants or loans to those providing courses.

The Manpower Services Commission's YTS Training for Skills can be particularly useful to most businesses. Under this scheme employers who agree to train more young people (16-year-old school leavers, unemployed 17-year-olds and disabled people up to 21-years-old), receive a grant of £1,950 per annum and a fee of £100 per annum for each trainee. Of the grant, £1,365 per annum (£26.25 a week) is to be paid to the trainee as an allowance. The employer must provide a minimum of two years of planned work experience and training, including a minimum of 13 weeks 'off-the-job' training or further education. There is no obligation to offer trainees permanent jobs at the end of their training. However, the procedure is complicated and 'Approved Training Organisation Status' has to be granted. Further information can be obtained from the Manpower Services Commission, YTS division.

14 SECURITY AND INSURANCE

● **88 How important is security?**

Losses which are incurred as a result of poor security can have a devastating effect on the profitability of your business. The main risks lie in assets that can be damaged or stolen, for example, your premises, equipment, stock or cash. The theft of information is a further risk. Computer files are particularly vulnerable to malicious damage as well as to theft or misuse.

To protect your business you must establish controls over your assets, your employees and any visitors. Failure to do so may lead to direct or indirect losses, such as the cost of replacing an asset and the inconvenience and loss of profits if operations are disrupted. Remember to include your accounting and other records in your security plans. Few, for example, could hope to collect all their outstanding debts if their sales ledger and copy invoices were lost; mailing lists are now a vital asset of many businesses and must also be protected.

The problems of business security are essentially the same as home security; the more valuable your possessions, the more careful your precautions must be. Even simple controls such as locking the storeroom, employing a doorman, counting the stock and examining equipment regularly, may reduce the likelihood of theft.

Do not go too far, however, and disrupt the efficiency of your operations. You must allow your staff access to assets they need for their jobs. Keep your security arrangements at a level which deters misuse but allows people to get on with their work.

Proper interviewing procedures (including taking up references) can reduce the risks from employees. Adequate supervision of your employees is vital. You must also make sure that visitors are not allowed free access to your premises. Insist that they are accompanied by an employee. Retail operations, particularly self-service stores, have special problems and may require the help of a crime-prevention specialist.

89 If I am insured do I need security precautions as well? ●

Insurance will rarely compensate for all the losses – in money and inconvenience – which theft or damage causes. Insurers will insist that you have a certain minimum level of security before they give or renew insurance cover. You may also be able to negotiate substantial savings on premiums if your security arrangements are better than average.

If you are in any doubt, imagine the worst; a fire, started deliberately, destroys your premises and all its contents. Your insurance may allow you to replace all the assets eventually but, when you start-up again, can you be sure that your customers have waited? Security cannot remove all risks but an attempt at prevention is surely preferable to the cure in these circumstances.

90 What should I insure against? ●

In four areas you have no choice but to insure. These are:
Employer's liability insurance – this covers the employer against liability for personal injury and disease sustained by an employee arising out of, or in the course of, their employment.
Public liability insurance – this covers the business for injury to people other than employees, on or off the premises.
National insurance contributions – you must pay these for yourself and your employees.
Vehicle insurance – you need at least third-party cover.

Other forms of insurance are not compulsory but it can be disastrous to gamble with too little insurance. It would be sensible to take out the following forms of insurance:
Insurance for premises and contents – to cover the risks of fire, flood, other natural hazards and burglary. Make certain that this will cover the current costs of replacement and repairs and the consequential losses – professional fees, wages of employees who are not working, etc. – as well as the loss of profits as a result of any hold-up in operations.

Insurance of personnel – the loss of services of key personnel through illness, injury or death can seriously damage a business. Insurance is particularly important for partnerships where the death of a partner means that his investment in the firm must be repaid to his estate (this type of difficulty can also be mitigated by a carefully constructed partnership agreement specifying repayment over a long period).

There are numerous other risks against which insurance can be obtained. You should consult your professional advisers on what is available and appropriate to your business. You may be able to save on insurance by shopping around, but do not economise on the level of cover. Use brokers and insurance companies with good reputations.

● **91   How does an approved pension plan benefit the company?**

There are two ways in which a pension plan can benefit the company:
– financially;
– employee relations.

'Exempt approved company pension schemes' offer the best tax planning opportunities for the company and the sole trader as contributions are tax-deductible.

Developing good employee/employer relations is essential to the smooth running of any organisation. To show the employees how much the company appreciates their service, you can start an approved pension scheme. There are many ways to do this. You can link the contribution to the employees' overall salary package or you can base it on a time scale, i.e. the pension scheme is open to all employees after their first year of service. You can structure the scheme on a sliding scale of contribution, rewarding different grades of personnel with different benefits of contributions. You can also offer them the opportunity of adding to their pension by paying in a regular percentage of their salary. This is known as Additional Voluntary Contribution. Should employees agree to do this, they can claim tax relief against their payments; however, the limit is 15% of their salary per annum and this includes any compulsory contributions.

Individual benefits to both directors and employees broadly include:

(a) a pension of up to two-thirds of their final salary;

(b) to elect to have part of the pension paid as a tax-free lump sum and the rest paid as a monthly or annual pension;

(c) should death occur prematurely, the widow would receive up to four-ninths of the final salary;

(d) a life assurance cover of up to four times the yearly salary.

Extra benefits can be written into the pension, for example, permanent health insurance cover.

Pension plans can also benefit the sole trader or partner. If you have regularly contributed to your own personal pension fund, you may be able to receive a loan; this would be based on a percentage of the annual premium paid. By paying into your pension fund each year, on retirement, an accumulated cash sum will have built up. The final amount of pension which you will receive depends on how much you have contributed, over what period of time, and the investment performance of your chosen pension fund.

A word of caution before you commit yourself either to an individual pension scheme or to an approved company pension scheme, do ensure that you can afford to pay the premiums.

15 YOUR LEGAL OBLIGATIONS

● **92 How does the law affect my business?**

Every business is subject to national and local legislation. Contravening the law can lead to fines, imprisonment, and even closure of your business. Defending an action can also use up a huge amount of your senior employees' time, as well as your own, and costs money directly in legal fees. Avoiding legal problems will contribute significantly to the profitability of your business.

You cannot hope to become an expert in the law: even if you are a qualified solicitor, you are unlikely to have the time to keep up with the developments which might affect your business.

In this book we can give only an introduction to the areas of law in which you may become involved while running your business. You should realise that because of the volume and complexity of legislation, you will need further information and advice to apply what we say to your particular circumstances.

● **93 In which areas do I have legal obligations?**

The law is changed frequently, almost daily in fact, and local laws vary greatly. But, in general, your legal obligations are to your employees, your customers and statutory bodies. You also have responsibilities not to cause nuisance, damage, pollution and so on to the community.

We can only give a brief description of the most important areas of law you are likely to encounter. Some statutes, the titles of which give an idea of their scope, are merely mentioned.

Your Employees

A person who has worked for an employer for thirteen weeks must be given a written statement of the terms and conditions under which he is employed.

You must calculate each employee's wages, PAYE income tax and National Insurance deductions; record wages deductions and pay them to the Collector of Taxes.

You are responsible for paying Employer's National Insurance Contributions and Statutory Sick Pay. You are also obliged to comply with the Equal Pay Act 1970, the Sex Discrimination Act 1975, the Race Relations Act 1976, the Health and Safety at Work Act 1974, the Factories Act 1961 and the Offices, Shops and Railway Premises Act 1963.

Your Customers

A series of Acts has been introduced to protect customers, based on the premise that the customer is the weaker party in the transaction. The major statute is the Sale of Goods Act 1979 which requires that any goods sold are of merchantable quality. Goods must also be fit for the purpose for which they are bought, provided that the buyer makes known the particular purpose, unless the seller can prove that the buyer did not rely on the seller's skill, knowledge or judgement. The Unfair Contact Terms Act 1977 specifies terms which may not be excluded by the contract.

Other relevant statutes here are the Trades Description Act 1968, the Fair Trading Act 1973, the Consumer Credit Act 1974 and the Data Protection Act 1984.

Statutory Bodies

Your obligations vary accordingly to the legal structure of your business, particularly the way in which you will pay tax on your income.

(a) Sole trader or Partnership. There are few legal requirements for setting up a business as a sole trader or in partnership. Principally you must display your own name(s) at your place of business and on your letterheading if business is carried out under another name. Your business will be taxed under the income tax legislation. You must also comply with VAT rules, including maintaining adequate accounting records.

You are not required to file annual accounts, although you will need them for taxation purposes.

You do, however, have unlimited liability for all the debts of the business: partners also accept unlimited liability for the debts and action of each other.

There is no legal requirement to have a written partnership agreement but it is highly advisable.

(b) Limited company. The greatest advantage offered by such a company is the limit on the shareholder's liability for the company's debts. At present he is only liable for any unpaid amount on his shareholding. In return, the company must file its accounts each year with the Registrar of Companies and these accounts must be audited. The company must also comply with the provisions of the Companies Acts, including maintaining adequate accounting records.

Your company's profits and gains are liable to corporation tax and the company must comply with VAT rules.

Local Authorities

These control planning permission, granting of licences to businesses that require them (e.g. street traders, cinemas, nurseries) and collecting rates.

● **94 Where can I find out about my obligations?**

The amount of legislation affecting a business is large and constantly changing, but there are many sources of information and advice to help you manage.

There are many books written for the layman which can give you a grounding in law for business and can be referred to as necessary. Loose-leaf publications which are amended regularly will help you keep up to date. Ask your solicitor to recommend appropriate books.

The Inland Revenue, Department of Trade and Industry, the Department of Employment and the Health and Safety Executive issue explanatory leaflets on aspects of the law for which they are responsible.

Keep in touch with your solicitor on a regular basis. He should be able to warn you of new legislation or regulations which might affect your business. Local Chambers of Commerce and Trade Associations often run seminars on significant new developments.

If you think you have a problem, take professional advice early on: in the long run you will probably save money by adopting this policy.

95 What can I do about taxation?

●

All business profits are subject to tax: your aim should be to pay only as much as is required by law. Tax legislation is extremely complex and becomes more so with each new Finance Act. It is an area in which you must involve your professional advisers, particularly your accountant.

As the owner of a business, you should be concerned with tax on your personal income and capital as well as tax on the business.

The subject of tax is too large to discuss in any detail in this book. The *Sunday Telegraph's* publication *101 Ways of Saving Tax* will answer many of your questions.

96 Should tax considerations influence my business planning?

●

Many of the decisions you take about your business will have tax consequences: it is vital that you take these into account before you commit yourself to any action. Think about the tax implications for both the business and you as an individual taxpayer. The purpose of tax planning is to take advantage of the concessions offered by the tax system.

The planning must start at the very beginning: the legal form you choose for your business will determine the nature of its taxation liabilities. Sole traders and partnerships pay income tax: this difference affects the rates of tax, the accounting periods to be taxed and the categories of expenses which may be set off against profits.

Your regular planning must ensure that you submit returns and claims and pay any tax due on time. There are penalties for failing to do this. Make sure that you have adequate records: many businesses have collapsed because there was no evidence to contest an estimate of their liability presented by the Revenue.

Take suitable advice at the right time so that your planning takes account of all the consequences of a decision. You may decide to do something which has less than optimum tax consequences if other benefits outweigh this consideration. You need to be able to compare the benefits of each course of action in monetary terms to do this.

16 EXTERNAL ADVICE

● **97　When do I need professional advice?**

When you have insufficient time and resources, when the experience and skills of yourself and your employees are inadequate or when you want an objective opinion. It is impossible to state categorically when you will need advice. It is safe to say that if you are in doubt, take advice. There is more chance of solving your problem effectively as well as economically, if you call an expert in sooner rather than later.

There are some vulnerable points in the life of a business when involving a professional adviser will be most advisable, if not essential, for example when:
- buying or setting up a business;
- selling part of your business or its assets, particularly if you are retiring;
- considering major organisational, market, locational and other changes;
- agreeing tax liabilities and planning for the business and for you;
- implementing a computer system;
- arranging finance;
- raising new finance (particularly if you decide to go to the Unlisted Securities Market or Stock Exchange).

Approaching a professional adviser is similar in many ways to consulting a doctor. If you and your business have regular check-ups with your advisers you may prevent problems from developing.

● **98　What professional advisers do I need?**

You may have skills which reduce your need for professional advisers. As the business grows, you will also probably bring in professionally qualified staff to work as employees. But at every stage of your business's development, you will want to consult an expert in a particular field or seek an independent opinion.

Most businesses need the following external advisers:

(a) An accountant. If you run a company, you are required by law to appoint an accountant who is qualified to audit your annual accounts. Whatever the legal status of your business you will need financial advice (e.g. taxation, funding, personal financial planning) and other business services (e.g. accounting, information technology, personnel, production and marketing consultancy) which accountants can now provide.

(b) A solicitor. There are many legal formalities and obligations which arise from running a business, particularly when you are starting up and buying or selling premises and assets. The advice you need may involve laws on companies, partnerships, sale of goods and contract, taxation, employment, insurance, social security; this is by no means an exhaustive list.

(c) Insurance broker. The range of insurance you need is large (see question 90). A broker can give you advice and save you the time required to shop around the insurance companies.

(d) Other specialists. You may need to call in other specialists from time to time to solve particularly difficult problems or to look at your operation as a whole. These include management consultants (who provide advice on every area of business, e.g. organisation, structure, production management, personnel, information technology, marketing and distribution) and consultants in particular industries (e.g. transportation, catering, engineering) or disciplines (e.g. surveyors, town planner, architects, estate agents).

● 99 How should I choose professional advisers?

You must remember, no matter how many professional advisers you appoint, that the final decisions about the future of your business are yours. It is essential, therefore, that you should have confidence in your advisers and not feel overawed by them.

Personal recommendation is probably the best method of choosing an adviser, preferably from an experienced business person; for example, if you like and respect your bank manager, ask him if he can recommend any solicitors and accountants. See several firms before making your choice: you need to form a close relationship with your advisers; personalities as well as skills can affect your choice. Most firms are willing to discuss the range of service and their approach with potential clients, without obligation or charge.

A smaller business will often benefit from picking advisers who are locally based. Area branches of professional societies (e.g. the Law Society or Institute of Chartered Accountants) will provide lists of members operating nearby.

Make sure the advisers you choose have experience in advising businesses and businessmen. Think about the development of your business: if you intend to expand consider what services you are likely to want in, say, two or even ten years time, and look for a solicitor or accountant who can deal with a larger business and who offers a wide range of related services. You will have to work closely with these people over the years and they will get to know a lot about your business; if you have to change advisers because they cannot keep pace with your business, you will have to pay for the new ones to familiarise themselves with your affairs.

100   What should I expect to pay for advice?

In general, accountants, solicitors and consultants charge on a time basis. Insurance brokers usually receive a commission from the insurance company and do not charge clients for advice. Your bank will charge interest on loans and overdrafts and a flat charge per item and service used. The bank manager will not usually charge for any advice he gives you.

Be prepared to shop around; the advisers will expect you to, they are aware of the need to charge competitively. Rates vary accordingly to area, size of practice, specialist services offered and the seniority of the staff involved and they change from year to year.

Price should not necessarily be your only criterion, but you will want to make sure you get value for your fees, so be aware of services other firms or banks are offering. Ask questions and let them know if you are unhappy with them: in short, treat them as you would your other suppliers. You may also want to ask the firm to tender for your business against others after a few years.

101   Where can I find out more about all of these topics?

The subject matter covered in this book is vast and our answers can only give an introduction to the problems. However, there are many sources of information and here we list a few of the most useful and readily available.

(a) Your professional advisers. There is no substitute for them. If you have regular contact with your advisers, they should also keep you up-to-date on new developments which will affect your business.

(b) Books and newspapers. Most of the questions raised have been subjects of books in their own right. Be cautious, because printed advice can go out-of-date fairly quickly. You must be aware of what is happening in your marketplace, so read newspapers and business and trade journals regularly.

The *Daily Telegraph* and *Sunday Telegraph* publish and regularly update a library of books tailored to the needs of the businessman, covering everything from the law to taking up a franchise – these books are a handy tool in running a business for profit. Details are available from The Publications Department, Telegraph Publications, 135 Fleet Street, London EC4P 4BL.

(c) Local chambers of commerce and trade associations. These often hold meetings and training sessions on topical matters. You will also gain from talking to other businessmen about their experiences.

(d) Government departments. These provide guidance notes on many areas of their responsibilities and will often give some advice.

(e) Training courses and seminars. These are held by colleges, professional advisers, local associations and privately-run organisations. They are often advertised in relevant journals and you may also get recommendations from your business acquaintances.

A range of business and personal finance books from Telegraph Publications

101 Ways Series:

101 Ways of Saving Tax
by Bill Packer of Chartered Accountants Touche Ross and Elaine Baker
Answers all your questions about tax and shows you how to cut your tax bills. Updated to include changes made in the 1986 Budget.
£1.95 p/b

101 Ways of Investing and Saving Money
by Alex Murray
A short and straightforward handbook to guide you through the maze of opportunities open to the investor. Updated to include changes made in the 1986 Budget.
£2.50 p/b

Family Money-Go-Round Series:

A Consumer's Guide to Air Travel
by Frank Barrett
The popular, value-for-money guide to the variety of cheap air fares on offer. Shows you how to choose your travel agent, with full details on bucket shops, pre-flight checks, passengers' rights and corporate travel.
£3.95 p/b

A Consumer's Guide to Leaving Money to Children
by John Turner of Peat, Marwick and Mitchell
An invaluable guide illuminating the complex tax position and discussing the ways in which assets can be passed on to children with maximum benefit. Gives details of the possibilities offered by deeds of covenant, gifts, businesses, shares, reversions, options and trusts.
£3.95 p/b

A Consumer's Guide to Holidays Abroad
by Frank Barrett
From a package tour to Benidorm to a self help safari on the banks of the Limpopo this book has the lot. Written by acknowledged expert on cheap air fares, Frank Barrett, this book will help you choose the right holiday.
£3.95 p/b

A Consumer's Guide to Lump-Sum Investment
by Diana Wright

A comprehensive guide telling you what sort of returns you should expect from your investment, the importance of tax regulations, what you can invest your money in and where to go for professional advice.

£5.95 p/b

Forthcoming titles in series:

Planning for Retirement
by Tony Levene

With the increasing scientific and medical knowledge, more and more people are able to enjoy a longer retirement. The guide sets out all the legal and practical matters to be considered when approaching retirement.

£5.95 p/b

Divorce and Separation
by Felicity White

This book provides clear and sensible advice on how to handle all the legal, financial and practical aspects of divorce and separation. It aims to minimise the complications of a difficult period by presenting the various approaches and pinpointing the most suitable courses of action.

£5.95 p/b

Business Enterprise Series:

How to Set Up and Run your Own Business

An essential handbook for those setting up or running a small business, containing contributions from leading professionals in the fields of commerce and finance. Now in its fifth successful edition with over 40,000 copies sold to date.

£4.95 p/b £9.95 h/b

How to Choose and Use Business Microcomputers and Software
by Paul Beck

A book to help you through the pitfalls of buying a microcomputer explained in clear and simple terms and packed with advice from users who have had experience of buying and living with systems.

£5.95 p/b, £9.95 h/b

126

Forthcoming titles in series:

Conference Organiser's Handbook
Edited by John Fenton
A step-by-step guide to planning and conducting a successful conference. It aims to minimise time and expenditure and ensure the smooth running of operations. It includes a detailed checklist of all points to be covered in advance and special case studies highlighting the pitfalls to be avoided.
£5.95 p/b

Building Your Business Series:

How to Win Profitable Business
by Tom Cannon
Concentrates on practical ideas and methods, which turned into action, result in full order books, a busy factory and workforce, and increased growth and profits.
£5.95 p/b

How to Manage Money
by G. D. Donleavy and M. Metcalf
A lucid and comprehensive guide on how to make your money work harder for you in business.
£5.95 p/b, £9.95 h/b

How to Manage People
by Ron Johnson
Contains everything you need to know about motivating your staff, getting the very best out of them and keeping them keen, efficient and happy.
£5.95 p/b, £9.95 h/b

Know Your Law
by Greville Janner
Provides all the practical answers to legal problems your business is likely to meet.
£5.95 p/b, £9.95 h/b

All books are available through leading bookshops, the Telegraph Bookshop at 130 Fleet Street or by post from Telegraph Publications, Daily Telegraph, 135 Fleet Street, London EC4P 4BL. If ordering by post, please add 55p postage and packing per book.

Forthcoming titles:

Stocks and Shares
by Roger Hardman
The recent publicity surrounding the flotation of many national and high street companies has called for a clear handbook to assist the first-time buyer in making his choice. Filled with useful hints, this new guide simplifies the whole process, and will be published to coincide with this Autumn's 'Big Bang' in the London Stock Market.
£5.95 p/b